THE

EVERYTHING®
ORGANIC
BABY MEALS
COOKBOOK

Welcome to the EVERYTHING Series!

These handy, accessible books give you all you need to tackle a difficult project, gain a new hobby, comprehend a fascinating topic, prepare for an exam, or even brush up on something you learned back in school but have since forgotten.

You can choose to read an Everything® book from cover to cover or just pick out the information you want from our four useful boxes: e-questions, e-facts, e-alerts, e-ssentials. We give you everything you need to know on the subject, but throw in a lot of fun stuff along the way, too.

We now have more than 400 Everything® books in print, spanning such wide-ranging categories as weddings, pregnancy, cooking, music instruction, foreign language, crafts, pets, New Age, and so much more. When you're done reading them all, you can finally say you know Everything®!

PUBLISHER Karen Cooper

MANAGING EDITOR, EVERYTHING® SERIES Lisa Laing

COPY CHIEF Casey Ebert

ASSISTANT PRODUCTION EDITOR Alex Guarco

ACQUISITIONS EDITOR Lisa Laing

SENIOR DEVELOPMENT EDITOR Brett Palana-Shanahan

EVERYTHING® SERIES COVER DESIGNER Erin Alexander

Visit the entire Everything® series at *www.everything.com*

THE
EVERYTHING®
ORGANIC BABY MEALS COOKBOOK

Avon, Massachusetts

An Everything® Series Book.
Everything® and everything.com® are registered trademarks of F+W Media, Inc.

Published by
Adams Media, a division of F+W Media, Inc.
57 Littlefield Street, Avon, MA 02322. U.S.A.
www.adamsmedia.com

Contains material adapted and abridged from *The Everything® Organic Cooking for Baby & Toddler Book* by Kim Lutz and Megan Hart, MS, RD, copyright ©
2008 by F+W Media, Inc., ISBN 10: 1-59869-926-1, ISBN 13: 978-1-59869-926-5.

ISBN 10: 1-4405-8722-1
ISBN 13: 978-1-4405-8722-1
eISBN 10: 1-4405-8723-X
eISBN 13: 978-1-4405-8723-8

Printed in the United States of America.

10 9 8 7 6 5 4 3 2 1

Cover images © StockFood/King, Dave; © StockFood/Cooke, Colin;
© StockFood/Lutterbeck, Barbara; © StockFood/Meier, Chris.

This book is available at quantity discounts for bulk purchases.
For information, please call 1-800-289-0963.

Contents

Introduction

New parents are faced with what seems like a million decisions to make. The choices surrounding how and what to feed your baby are some of the most important decisions that you will make. The foods that you choose to provide will help your child's body and mind grow and develop to her fullest potential. How those foods came from the farm to the table will greatly impact not only the health of your baby, but also the health of our planet. Choosing to feed your baby and toddler organic food is one choice that is good for your child, your family, and your world.

Luckily, this serious decision is also delicious! *The Everything® Organic Baby Meals Cookbook* contains more than 250 recipes that will delight your baby, from first foods to organic family dining. How can preparing Pear Purée, Blueberry Pancakes, and Cherry Apple Coconut Rice Pudding help save the world? As this book explains, organic farming is better for the environment. Organic farmers do not use toxic pesticides, insecticides, and synthetic fertilizers. Instead, organic farmers use natural methods—including crop rotation, natural fertilizers, and letting fields lie fallow—to allow nature's bounty to shine through. Organic livestock are given access to fresh air, fresh water, and a healthy diet; they are not given routine doses of antibiotics or warehoused in cramped quarters. Organic farming contributes to cleaner air, water, and soil. The simple act of choosing organic means that you are also helping ensure that the natural environment is protected.

Since the vast majority of a baby's nutrition in the first year of life comes from breast milk or formula, babies have the opportunity to learn about different tastes and textures during their early experiences with food. This cookbook provides recipes for those basic purées and sets the groundwork for introducing a variety of tastes, flavors, and combinations to help babies develop into healthy eaters as they grow.

These recipes emphasize natural sweeteners and seasonings rather than relying on refined sugars and salt. Developing good eating habits begins right from your baby's first experience with food. Your baby will come to know food with its true flavors shining through rather than being masked by unhealthy additives.

Many children go through phases when their palates become more limited. For pickier little ones, there are a variety of options that provide sound nutrition in the guise of a treat. There are cool sorbets, fruity smoothies, and fun dips to enchant even the most reluctant eater. Even birthday cakes are given the organic once-over in this family-friendly cookbook.

This cookbook can help you set the table for healthy eating habits that will last a lifetime. Organic eating can also help you contribute to a healthier planet. Enjoy watching your baby grow into a healthy, happy, organic child!

In closing here is one important note: When reading the recipes in this book please remember that while each individual ingredient does not have the word *organic* before it, it is assumed that you will be using only organic foods for these recipes.

CHAPTER 1

Why Organic?

With so many choices facing new parents, why is it important to consider feeding your baby organic food? Because your child will undergo so many significant changes during the first three years of life, it is imperative that he receives the best tools to grow and develop. Food that has been organically grown and produced provides just what your baby needs to grow from a tiny, smiling bundle to an active, engaged toddler without any dangerous chemicals to get in the way of that healthy development.

What Is Organic?

At its core, organic food is food that has been grown and produced as close as possible to the way that nature intended. Organic produce is grown without the aid of pesticides, herbicides, or synthetic fertilizers. Because organic livestock does not receive routine doses of antibiotics, the animals have living conditions that promote good health, including adequate space, fresh air, fresh water, and healthy feed. Furthermore, genetically modified organisms (GMOs), synthetic hormones, and irradiation are not allowed in organic agricultural products. Not only is organic food grown in accordance with organic practices, but the organic commitment also continues all the way from field to store.

Since 2002, the United States Department of Agriculture (USDA) has overseen the national organic program in the United States. The USDA has instituted an extensive set of rules that dictate what is allowable and what is prohibited in organic agricultural products for food and nonfood use. The USDA also oversees third-party certifiers, which ensure that the rules are followed by organic producers. There are three levels to the USDA organic labeling program:

- Products labeled "100 Percent Organic" are made entirely from organic ingredients or components.
- Products that are made up of at least 95 percent organic ingredients or components, and have remaining ingredients that are approved for use in organic products, can display the "USDA Organic" seal.
- Products that are made up of at least 70 percent organic ingredients or components can list "organic" before those ingredients on their ingredient lists.

Alert

The USDA does not require third-party certification of organic products from farmers or distributors who sell less than $5,000 of goods per year. However, if these exempt producers attempt to misuse the "organic" label, and are caught, they are subject to a significant penalty.

Why Is Organic Important?

As a new parent, there is nothing as important as taking good care of your child. There are many ways to ensure your child's good health, happiness, and safety. Buying and preparing organic foods contributes to these goals in several ways.

Organics Are Good for Your Baby's Body

A variety of wholesome, nutritious foods is what your baby needs to develop in both body and mind. Chemicals, in the form of added artificial flavorings, dyes, pesticide and herbicide residues, and hydrogenated fats, do nothing to promote good health, and can even detract from it. Organically grown and produced food is free of these chemicals, leaving only the good taste and nutrition that nature intended.

Babies and children who are fed an organic diet are not over-exposed to antibiotic residue in their food, either. Animals are healthier when farmed organically, because they have adequate access to fresh air, appropriate diet, and outdoor space. Therefore, the need for antibiotic overuse is eliminated. (According to USDA rules, organic meat must be antibiotic-free.)

Organics Are Better for the Planet

Taking care of the world that your baby will inherit is also good parenting. Organic farming is based on keeping the soil healthy through natural means like rotating crops, letting fields lie fallow, and using natural fertilizing methods rather than spraying on toxic pesticides and herbicides that can run off into water supplies and contaminate the soil.

Organic livestock farms provide adequate room for the animals and do not rely on factory-farm overcrowding and the waste-disposal issues that accompany it. Because organic livestock is fed an organic diet, that also means fewer synthetic pesticides and herbicides are used in the crops that are dedicated for their feed.

Increased soil fertility is another bonus of organic farming. Organic farmers use natural methods to replenish the soil so they don't strip the earth of its nutrients by overfarming. Conscientious stewardship of the soil is a hallmark of organic farming as it is the only way for the organic farmer to reap another year's yield.

Top Twenty Heroic Organic Foods

Although the ideal is to provide your baby with a completely organic diet, there are several reasons why that might not be possible all the time. For one, organics can be more expensive than conventional foods, and some family budgets cannot support buying all organic all the time. Another reason is that, depending on the season, fresh, locally grown organic produce might not be available.

Choosing Pesticide-Free Organic Produce

When deciding which organics to choose, the relative pesticide load of each conventionally grown produce variety should be factored into the decision. The Environmental Working Group ranks produce based on its pesticide load. The fruits and vegetables at the top of the list are those that, when produced conventionally, carry the heaviest load of pesticides. The following list includes the twenty fruits and vegetables for which it is most important to buy organic. To see an updated list, visit the Environmental Working Group's website, *www.foodnews.org.*

1. Apples	11. Snap peas (imported)
2. Strawberries	12. Potatoes
3. Grapes	13. Hot peppers
4. Celery	14. Blueberries (domestic)
5. Peaches	15. Lettuce
6. Spinach	16. Kale/collard greens
7. Sweet bell peppers	17. Plums
8. Nectarines	18. Cherries
9. Cucumbers	19. Nectarines (domestic)
10. Cherry tomatoes	20. Pears

Even though most people wash their produce before eating or cooking, some pesticide residue can remain. This list considers common washing practices and the residue that remains after washing.

Milk

USDA-certified milk is produced at farms that follow all of the rules and regulations for organic dairy farming. These rules include feeding the cows an organic diet, using organic fertilizer, allowing the cows adequate space and access to fresh air, and restricting medications. Depending on economic circumstances, milk can cost up to twice as much as conventional milk. If that extra expense puts buying milk out of reach for your family 100 percent of the time, there are other options.

 Fact

Some milk is fortified with omega-3 fatty acids. Omega-3 is an essential fatty acid that is required for healthy growth. Regular intake of omega-3 can protect you from various diseases and helps you reduce incidences of heart disease, certain types of cancer, and arthritis.

Hormone-free milk is a category that falls somewhere between organic and conventional milk. The hormone rBGH (recombinant bovine growth hormone) is a substance that is given to cows to increase their milk production. It can, however, increase the chance of infection and other health problems in the cows that receive it. The idea behind rBGH-free or hormone-free milk is that cows are healthier without the hormone, and therefore require less medical care. Specifically, it is believed that these cows will need fewer antibiotics, and therefore there will be less chance of antibiotic residue in the milk supply from rBGH-free cows. For more information on rBGH or other synthetic hormones, visit *www.organicconsumers.org* or *www.centerforfoodsafety.org*.

Genetically Modified Organisms

The term *genetically modified organism* (GMO) is usually applied to food crops that have had their genetic material engineered to incorporate the genetic material of another species. Farmers have always taken advantage of cross-breeding, creating hybrids within a species and taking advantage of genetic mutations. The navel orange, for instance, is a mutation that has been commercially farmed for generations. However, there is some controversy over whether introducing the genetic material of different species into seeds or plants is safe. Studies are currently underway to help us better understand whether GMOs are safe for the human body and/or the environment.

All organics are GMO-free, but so are many conventional fruits and vegetables. If you are trying to buy GMO-free, look for a label stating that the product doesn't use any genetically modified ingredients. According to the USDA, three crops make up the majority of GMOs in the United States:

- Corn
- Cotton
- Soybeans

For more detailed information, visit *www.ers.usda.gov/topics/farm-practices-management/biotechnology*.

Choosing to buy food products that are formulated with the organic versions of these ingredients, or that avoid using these ingredients, will greatly decrease the occurrence of GMOs in your diet. For example, a juice drink that is free of corn syrup is much more likely to be free of GMOs than one that contains corn syrup.

How to Create a Healthy Organic Table

As with most everything, in feeding your family, variety is the spice of life. Serving seasonal produce in a variety of colors with a wide range of whole grains and protein sources ensures that your family receives the full spectrum of nutrients that bodies need to function at their best. The USDA's "Dietary Guidelines for Americans 2005" emphasizes this variety by recommending that Americans over age two follow the food pyramid guidelines.

These recommendations emphasize:

- Eating a variety of fruits, vegetables, and legumes in a variety of colors
- Eating a variety of whole-grain products
- Consuming low-fat or fat-free dairy products or equivalent milk products (Remember, these recommendations are for people over age two. Until age two, children should be fed whole milk.)
- Limiting added sugar, salt, and saturated fat, and avoiding trans fats

For a personal food pyramid, visit *www.ChooseMyPlate.gov*.

Fresh, Frozen, or Canned? What to Choose?

The decision to promote your baby's good health and development by providing organic food is a great first step on the road to healthy eating for your family and better health for the planet. More decisions await, however. Is it always best to choose fresh produce? The answer to that is—it depends.

Fresh, Seasonal Produce

The ideal would be to have a wide variety of fresh, organic produce available at an affordable price all year long. There are a number of avenues to procure fresh, organic produce. One is your local farmers' market or farm stand. In rural communities, farm stands on the side of the road sell the fresh-picked fruits and vegetables that were growing on the farm just that morning. Some farms even offer you-pick-it opportunities to bring the consumer closer to the land. Nothing could be fresher than picking a bushel of apples off the tree and bringing them home to eat and cook right away. In urban communities around the country, the farm comes to them. Farmers awaken in the pre-dawn hours to bring fresh-picked produce to urban neighborhoods for same-day purchase. Not only does the farmers' market shopper get the chance to purchase fresh, in-season produce, but she also gets the chance to ask questions directly to the farmer about growing practices, thereby getting the best information about possible chemical exposure or organic status.

 **Essential**

Organic produce is becoming increasingly available at well-stocked grocery stores. Demand dictates what grocery stores stock, so if you want to see more organics at your local market, be sure to ask the manager. By letting management know that organics will be purchased and not go to waste, you are likely to see a positive response to your requests.

Another option that is gaining popularity is community-supported agriculture (CSA). The basic idea behind a CSA is that the consumer helps support the costs of growing the fruits and vegetables. Consumers purchase a "share" or membership in the CSA, and then pay either by the week or by the growing season in order to receive a box or bag of fresh fruits and vegetables. The CSA model has helped many small farmers to continue to farm. The revenue gained from the membership or share fees goes toward buying seed and the initial costs of planting, so the farmer does not have to wait for the harvest to collect money. This model allows the consumer to play a more active role in the food-production process. An interesting facet of the CSA idea is that usually you will receive a box or bag of produce, but won't know beforehand what you are going to get. This element of surprise can keep cooking exciting when you receive a previously unknown root vegetable or variety of green.

Organic produce can be as close as your own backyard. Growing organic fruits and vegetables can be as easy as setting up some pots with organic soil and seed on your balcony or in your backyard. This can be an inexpensive option to ensure that the organic tomatoes you love are readily at hand. You can also turn an area of your yard into an organic garden plot. This can take longer, as you often have to remedy past soil contamination problems, but can be well worth the effort if you have the space and the inclination. The Internet, libraries, and bookstores are full of resources to help the interested gardener. For instance, check out *www.organichomegardener.com* and *Organic Gardener* magazine. Don't be afraid to ask for help at your local gardening center, either.

It can be difficult to know what produce is in season in each region of the country. The Natural Resources Defense Council has made it much easier to figure out when to expect Brussels sprouts in your community. Visit *www.nrdc.org* and check out the "What's Fresh Near You" service. It lets you know what's growing in your region of the country.

Fabulous Frozen Food

One of the best ways to take advantage of each growing season is to freeze extra fruits or vegetables for later use. Whether you cook up an extra-large batch of purées, or you wash and freeze an extra quart of blueberries, you will be happy to have the taste of late summer when the leaves are falling off the trees. Frozen fruits and vegetables can be used for up to six months, and meats can be used for up to three months. That means that May's plums can still be enjoyed in October. Freezing can allow you to store extra produce for future use, extending the life of fruits and vegetables that would otherwise go to waste. If you have five very ripe bananas, but will only be able to eat one in the next day, peel the others and freeze them for use in smoothies later.

Because most commercially frozen organic produce is flash-frozen immediately after picking, most of the nutrients are preserved. Although your supermarket might have fresh organic berries in December, they could have traveled halfway around the world before they came to your community. Buying frozen fruit that was grown and frozen in your state will have used considerably fewer resources than the out-of-season fresh option. You can use these frozen fruits and vegetables to add variety when there are only limited fresh choices available in your region of the country.

 Alert

Most vegetables and fruits are picked, packaged, and frozen within six hours of being harvested. These frozen vegetables can have more of certain vitamins than the fresh ones that you buy at your grocery store, as that produce may have been harvested five or more days before it reached you.

What about Canned?

Canned beans, fruits, and vegetables can provide convenience and nutrition. Although dry beans can be an extremely affordable protein source, sometimes busy parents don't have the time necessary to soak and cook the beans before preparing them in their dinner entrée. Canned beans are a good source of protein, iron, and fiber. They also only require draining and rinsing before they're ready to incorporate in a salad, soup, or casserole.

 Fact

Canned tomatoes and tomato sauces are among the best sources of lycopene. Lycopene, found in red-pigmented fruits and vegetables like tomatoes, may help prevent certain cancers. The heat from the canning process allows the lycopene in the tomatoes to be better absorbed in the body.

Many canned fruits, like pineapple, mandarin oranges, and tomato products, are good sources of vitamin C. They are great to have on hand to use in a wide range of recipes. Canned tomatoes and tomato sauces are also a great source of lycopene, an antioxidant. Using canned pumpkin instead of cooking a whole pumpkin can mean the difference between having quick, nutrition-packed muffins or doing without. The important thing is to ensure that your family is eating a diet rich in a variety of fruits and vegetables. Using a combination of fresh, frozen, and canned can help promote your family's good health.

CHAPTER 2

Introduction to Feeding

Y ou are starting on the path to feeding your child organically. Where do you begin? This chapter takes you through the first few years of feeding your child. You will learn about breastfeeding and formula feeding your infant, how to determine when your child is ready for solid foods, and how to gradually introduce foods to your child in a safe manner. This chapter will also help you to stock your kitchen and pantry so you are ready to prepare fun and healthful organic meals and snacks for your child.

Breast Milk: The Ultimate Organic Food

As a parent, you have the privilege of feeding your child. There are many choices that a parent has in feeding their family and at times it can be overwhelming. Breastfeeding is one choice that parents may make to help their child get started on the organic eating path. Overall, the number of mothers choosing to breastfeed is on the rise.

Although breastfeeding is wonderful and natural, breastfeeding successfully can be hard. Many people struggle with achieving a solid breastfeeding schedule. Gather people around you who support breastfeeding and expect to need their help in order to be successful. Contact the local chapter of La Leche League early in your pregnancy to begin to develop your support system for breastfeeding.

The Gold Standard

The benefits of breastfeeding are thoroughly researched and well known in the medical community. There are emotional, physical, and cognitive benefits to breastfeeding. Breastfeeding promotes infant-maternal bonding through close contact and changes to a mother's hormone levels during breastfeeding. There is very little that compares to the feeling of nurturing your child through breastfeeding. The convenience and low cost of breastfeeding is also a plus for many mothers.

Breast milk has many fantastic health benefits. The nutritional composition of breast milk is superior to formula. Breast milk is the ultimate "gold standard" for infant feeding. Commercially available infant formulas all strive to be as close to breast milk as possible. However, there are many reasons why breast milk is the best choice for infant nutrition. First, the composition of breast milk is very easy for your infant to digest and absorb. The protein available in breast milk is easily and readily utilized by growing infants. Additionally, the calcium and phosphorous in breast milk is easily used by your infant's rapidly growing bones.

Beyond Nutrition

Beyond nutrition, breast milk has other benefits for your child. Breast milk contains antibodies. Antibodies are molecules in the immune system that help children fight infections. In developed countries, the effects on the immune system from these antibodies might be seen in the following ways: lower rates of diarrhea, lower rates of infections in the lungs and respiratory system, and lower rates of ear and urinary tract infections. There is also some evidence to suggest that breastfeeding improves cognitive development in infants. This information does not mean that your breast-fed infant will not have any of these problems; however, the risk of them is less. If they do occur, they might be less severe.

It is recommended that breast milk be the sole source of nutrition until six months of age and be offered in addition to solid food until at least the age of one year. Breast milk provides all the nutrients, vitamins, minerals, and fluids that your young infant needs to grow and develop. However, there are a few exceptions to this rule. Most babies receive a single dose of vitamin K at birth to help with blood clotting. According to the American Academy of Pediatrics, most exclusively breastfed infants also need an additional 200–400 international units of vitamin D. Recommendations about iron and fluoride are specific to your individual feeding plan and water source for your family. Please discuss the vitamins that your child may benefit from with your pediatrician or dietitian and decide what is right for your baby.

 Fact

There is some research that indicates that your child may have a lower risk of chronic diseases if breastfed as an infant. It is possible that breastfeeding can lower your child's risk of certain gastrointestinal diseases, certain lymphomas, and some types of diabetes.

When Formula Is Best

There are many situations in life that prevent families from being able to choose breastfeeding as their child's primary source of nutrition. Many times, parents choose to feed their infant with commercially prepared infant formulas due to certain medical and social situations. Parents should not feel guilty about this decision. It is important for each family to make the best decision for their own unique needs. Fortunately, there are many excellent options for feeding your child.

Types of Formula

Most commercially prepared infant formulas are split into three general categories based on the type of protein that is in the formula. The categories are whole-protein formula, partially digested protein formula, and free amino acid–based formula.

What does this mean? Proteins are made up of many small amino acids. Protein helps your baby to grow. The type of protein can make a formula easier or harder for your baby to digest. Most infants tolerate whole proteins without problems and grow nicely on a standard cow's milk infant formula. There are different medical situations that would make a child need a protein that is easier to digest. In the partially digested or free amino acid formulas, the protein is partially or completely broken down for your child. These formulas tend to be easier to digest, but not every baby needs these special formulas. This book will focus on the use of standard whole-protein formulas since these are the most common. Talk with your pediatrician or dietitian about the possibility that your child may need a more specialized formula, such as a partially digested formula or a free amino acid formula.

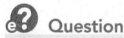 Question

What formula should you choose?
Going into the formula aisle can be overwhelming. There are so many types of formulas all made by different companies. How do you choose? It is important to know that all commercially prepared infant formulas must meet basic federal guidelines regarding composition. They vary slightly in how they achieve these guidelines but all formulas—except low-iron formulas—are adequate to support the growth and development of infants.

Standard Infant Formulas

The most common and widely used formula is a standard infant formula with iron. These formulas have been made with whole proteins that have not been broken down or predigested for your child. They are typically made from protein derived from cow's milk or from soy protein. Certain formulas indicate that they are made from "comfort proteins," and these are also included in this class of standard infant formulas. These formulas process their protein a little differently, but they are still whole-protein sources.

Cow's milk protein infant formulas with iron are the most widely used formulas overall. The cow's milk protein in infant formulas is not the same thing as whole milk. It has been altered by adding vegetable oils and carbohydrate sources to provide balanced and age-appropriate nutrition for your infant. This protein blend is readily bioavailable to your child, meaning that your child can absorb this protein better for growth and development.

Soy Protein Formulas

Soy protein formulas with iron use the protein from a soy protein isolate that is fortified with different amino acids and iron. Soy formulas differ slightly from the standard cow's milk protein formula. It is rare that children need a soy-based formula. Soy formulas meet all the federal guidelines for infant formulas; however, the nutrients are not always in the most bioavailable form for your child.

There are certain medical conditions that require an infant to need a soy formula. Notably, if you suspect that your child has an allergy to cow's milk protein, the recommendation is to *not* change him to a soy protein formula. If your child is allergic to cow's milk protein, there is a high chance that he could be allergic to soy formula as well. The current recommendation from the American Academy of Pediatrics is to change the diet of a child with cow's milk protein allergy to a special protein made from free amino acids. This means the formula is totally predigested for your child. These are highly specialized formulas and only available by prescription.

Organic Formula

The demand for organic products continues to increase. This has also led to an increased demand for organic infant formulas. Many formula companies are now producing infant formulas made from organic materials. Organic formulas are available in both cow's milk protein formula and soy-based formulas.

These formulas are typically certified organic in accordance with USDA regulations. To be certified USDA Organic and display the USDA Organic seal, a product must contain at least 95 percent organic ingredients by weight. Moreover, they are often certified organic by Quality Assurance International (QAI). The ingredients in these infant formulas are produced without using pesticides, added growth hormones, or antibiotics. These formulas meet the same standards as other formula for infant nutrition. They include all the components that a young infant needs to grow and thrive.

When Is My Baby Ready for Solids?

It is recommended that breast milk or infant formula with iron be the sole source of nutrition until age six months. However, some people feel that their baby is ready to start solids as early as four months. Discuss your baby's feeding plan with your pediatrician or dietitian before starting solids.

The rule of thumb in deciding if your child is ready for solids is to watch your baby, not the calendar. Your baby will let you know when she is ready for solids with some simple cues. Feeding before these cues are shown can lead to overfeeding and obesity.

Watch Your Baby, Not the Calendar

Your baby will give cues to show you she is ready for solids:

- Baby can hold her neck steady
- Baby can sit with support
- Baby can swallow nonliquid foods
- She opens her mouth for food
- She leans forward to indicate hunger
- She leans back to show that she is satisfied

- She can draw in her lip as the spoon is removed from her mouth
- She can move food from the front to the back of the mouth

If your baby is showing these signs, he or she is ready to begin taking solids. As your child moves through the next six months of the first year, you will have the joy of teaching your child how to eat independently. Get your bibs and washcloths or drop cloths ready! Watching your child begin to experience food is a fun time.

Advancing Your Baby's Diet

As your child becomes more comfortable with being fed, you can start teaching him to self-feed. Here are some skills to work on the next six months of your child's life:

- Self-feeding with easy, soft finger foods
- Trying to use a sippy cup at six to eight months
- Holding his own bottle or cup
- Exposing him to different textures and flavors

Feeding your child is a wonderful way to bond with him and teach him all about flavor and textures. Never force-feed your child. Your job as a parent is to provide healthful options at meal and snack times. Allow your child to determine how much to eat of the foods that you offer.

How Much Food Should You Offer Your Child?

Every baby is unique. Each child advances at his or her own pace and time. Pay attention to your child's developmental stages and feed according to those skills. The amounts of food to offer your child given in this chapter are just a guide; each baby is different and your child may eat more or less than these recommended servings. Your job as a parent is only to offer the foods to your child. Pay attention to your child's feeding cues to know if she is finished eating or wants to continue to eat. Here is a guide for feeding advancement for the first year through toddler eating.

Birth to Four Months

Your baby should have a rooting reflex, which means that he turns his head toward you to eat. Your baby should also be able to suck and swallow liquids. Babies at this age should only be taking breast milk or iron-fortified infant formula. His schedule will be sporadic but overall his daily intake of breast milk or iron-fortified infant formula should be 21 to 24 ounces. Your infant does not need any additional water or juice—these are not needed in the first year of life. Breast milk or formula can provide all the hydration that your infant needs under age one.

Five Months

Your baby can hold her neck up and begin to sit with support. At this age, babies should be drinking only breast milk or iron-fortified infant formula. She will begin to spread out her feeding and feed about four to six times per day. The overall goal amount of breast milk or iron-fortified infant formula is about 24 to 34 ounces per day.

Six to Seven Months

Your baby is starting to reach and grasp for objects. He has also been experimenting with moving his jaw up and down. Your infant should continue to drink 24 to 34 ounces of breast milk or iron-fortified infant formula per day, but this is the appropriate time to introduce iron-fortified rice cereal in addition to breast milk or formula. Your baby may eat about 4 tablespoons per day of cereal. Only introduce rice cereal with a spoon, as it is not appropriate to put rice cereal in a baby's bottle. You can also begin to introduce 4 tablespoons of vegetables and 4 tablespoons of fruits per day. Only introduce one new food at a time and wait four to seven days between each new food to monitor your child for potential allergies.

Eight to Nine Months

Your baby can now sit alone without support. She is developing her pincher grasp and can pick up small items with her thumb and finger. She is getting better at chewing, so you can begin to move away from all-puréed foods to a more mashed food consistency. She should drink 24 to 34 ounces of breast milk or iron-fortified infant formula per day. She can continue with the grain cereals, fruits, and vegetables and may take about ¼ to ½ cup of each of these per day. It is now appropriate to begin to introduce some soft meat purées. If her pincher grasp is ready, go ahead and give her some soft finger foods such as soft crackers, toast, cereal Os, or teething biscuits.

Ten to Twelve Months

Time to work on independent feeding! Your baby can now begin to hold a cup and will be interested in playing with food and self-feeding. He should still continue to drink 24 to 34 ounces of breast milk or iron-fortified infant formula per day. You can begin to offer small amounts of these in a sippy cup. Fruit juice can also be offered but your child should only have 4 ounces of juice per day. Juice can contribute to overfeeding and obesity, so be careful not to offer more than the recommended amount. Continue to expand the variety of cereals, fruits, vegetables, meats, soft breads, and finger foods. Babies will take about ¼- to ½-cup servings of each of these per day at this age.

Over Twelve Months

Your child has now been introduced to all the types of food groups. The goal is to continue to offer your child and your family a wide variety of textures, tastes, and food experiences. Playing with food is a normal and developmentally appropriate way to learn to accept new and different foods. Encourage playing with food.

Specific amounts of food that your child should eat are hard to prescribe. Toddlers' eating is sporadic and unpredictable. Children have days that they eat large amounts and days that they just pick at food. This is normal. Over time, your child will get the nutrients that she needs to grow.

Looking Forward: Toddler and Preschool Patterns and Portions

Here are some guidelines on toddler eating portions, but keep in mind that every child is different. Notice that their serving sizes are much smaller than adult portions.

GRAINS AND BREADS: 6 SERVINGS PER DAY
- Serving size: ¼ to ½ slice of bread or ½ cup of grain
- *Example:* 1 to 2 slices of bread + 1 cup of cereal per day

VEGETABLES: 3 SERVINGS PER DAY
- Serving size: ¼ to ⅓ cup
- *Example:* ½ cup cooked vegetables + ¼ cup of beans

FRUITS: 2 SERVINGS PER DAY
- Serving size: ⅓ cup
- *Example:* ⅓ cup of apple + ½ a banana

MILK: 2 SERVINGS PER DAY
- Serving size: 8 ounces of milk or 1 cup yogurt
- *Example:* 8 ounces whole milk + 1 (8 ounce) yogurt
- The goal is to transition to whole milk at one year old. Toddlers should stay on whole milk until the age of two and then can be switched to a lower-fat milk. Toddlers need two servings of dairy per day, or about 16 ounces. If your child cannot tolerate dairy, they should eat two servings of calcium- and vitamin D–fortified dairy substitute.

PROTEIN: 2 SERVINGS PER DAY

- Serving size: 1 to 2 ounces meat, 1 egg, ½ cup beans or tofu
- *Example:* 1 egg + 2 tablespoons tofu at lunch + 2 table-spoons meat at dinner

Children also need adequate amounts of zinc and protein in their diet. These nutrients can be obtained from two servings per day of meat, bean, or legume protein sources. Serving sizes for this age group are about 1 to 4 tablespoons of meat, and ½ cup of beans or legumes.

 Fact

Children under the age of two need to get a high percentage of their calories from fat for adequate brain development. For this reason, you should not limit the fat your child consumes under the age of two. Choose healthy fats from avocados, olive oil, and canola oil. For children over the age of two, you can begin to lower fat in the diet but children should never be on an extremely low-fat diet.

How Do I Safely Feed My Child?

When your child is showing all the developmental signs that he is ready for feeding, it is time to begin. It is such an exciting time in your child's life. You, as a parent, get to introduce your child to a whole new part of life—eating solid food. It is important that you do this in a safe manner.

Choking

Choking is a concern for every parent, but there are steps that you can take to prevent choking. Always watch your child when he is eating or playing around food. Do not allow your child to run around with food in his mouth. Your child should be seated and supervised for all meals and snacks. Make sure all items that your child could choke on are out of reach. And, most important, learn how to help your child if he is choking. Most community hospitals teach parents' first aid and CPR classes.

 Alert

According to the Center for Disease Control and Prevention, thousands of children visit the emergency each year due to choking. In fact, in the year 2000, there were 17,500 visits to the emergency room due to choking. Sixty percent of those visits were caused by children choking on food.

There are a handful of foods that are dangerous due to the high likelihood that your child could choke on them. The American Academy of Pediatrics recommends that all children under the age of four years old should avoid the following food items:

- Hot dogs
- Nuts and seeds (they recommend children be seven years old for nuts)
- Chunks of meat or cheese
- Whole grapes
- Hard, gooey, or sticky candy
- Popcorn
- Chunks of peanut butter
- Raw vegetables
- Raisins
- Chewing gum

Allergy Prevention

A food allergy is a reaction by your body's immune system to a food that it thinks is a threat. It is an "overreaction" of the immune system. The specific reactions range from rashes or hives to trouble breathing.

The eight most common food allergies are milk, egg, peanut, wheat, soy, tree nuts, fish, and shellfish. Some people have allergies to more than one of these top allergens. It is possible for your child to outgrow their allergies by the age of three. The only preventive measure to take for food allergies is total avoidance of the allergen; the only treatment is medication to help if a child is accidentally exposed to allergenic food.

 **Essential**

Research presented in the *Journal of Pediatrics* indicates that 4–6 percent of children have documented food allergies. Food allergies appear to be on the rise. More and more families are adjusting their dietary habits due to food allergies. These changes can be minor inconveniences or major life changes depending on the number and severity of food allergies.

There are steps that you can take to potentially decrease the chance that your child will develop food allergies. The current recommendation from the American Academy of Pediatrics is to exclusively breastfeed for the first six months of life to decrease their exposure to allergens. If breastfeeding is not possible, the recommendation is to exclusively formula feed and delay introduction of solids until the age of six months. In addition, it is recommended to not introduce cow's milk or egg yolks before the age of one year. If there is a family history of food allergies or atopic disease (e.g., hay fever, asthma, eczema), the recommendation is to further delay the introduction of eggs until the age of two and to wait until the age of three to introduce peanuts, tree nuts, fish, and seafood.

Some families, after consulting with their pediatrician, will begin to introduce solids to their infant as early as four months of age. This cookbook does include recipes for infants at this age to show how to introduce solids appropriately. If you start solids at this age, your child should be meeting the developmental milestones to support taking in solid foods. Take your time introducing food to your child. Eating is a new experience and there is no need to rush into offering a huge variety of foods to a very young infant.

Your child's first food should be a prepared iron-fortified infant rice cereal. This is a very hypoallergenic food. Take your time introducing new foods to look for signs of a food allergy. It is important to only introduce one new food at a time. It is recommended that you wait four to seven days after introducing one food before you introduce another. In those four to seven days, you should be watching your child for signs of food allergies. Look for signs such as itching, burning around the mouth, runny nose, skin rash, hives, diarrhea, vomiting, and trouble breathing. Once your child has tolerated a food, it is then acceptable to mix that food with another food that has also been established to be tolerated.

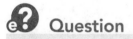 **Question**

I think my child has a food allergy. What should I do?
You and your pediatrician will need to decide how you are going to limit your child's exposure to high-allergen foods. If you suspect allergies in your child, see a pediatric allergist who is trained to identify true food allergies in your child.

Nitrates
What are nitrates? Nitrates are molecules that are comprised of nitrogen and oxygen. They are naturally found in the produce and in the water that people drink. As part of a balanced diet in adults, these products are not harmful. Nitrates can be harmful to young infants. The American Academy of Pediatrics (AAP) cautions parents about the risks of nitrate poisoning in infants.

Nitrate poisoning causes your baby to have high levels of methemoglobin in their bodies. Why is this a problem? If there is too much methemoglobin in the blood, oxygen has a hard time reaching your baby's cells. Cells need oxygen to function. This syndrome is sometimes called "blue baby" syndrome since baby's skin turns slightly blue due to lack of oxygen. Although rare, this can be a serious and life-threatening condition.

The highest risk for babies to develop nitrate poisoning is from well water with high levels of nitrates. Do not use well water unless it has been tested for nitrates. The concentration should be should be less than 10 parts per million (ppm). Another risk factor involves certain types of produce that can be high in nitrates due to the soil that they are grown in. These vegetables are spinach, beets, broccoli, and carrots. The AAP cautions parents against making their own baby food using these vegetables for infants under six months of age. Many commercial makers of baby food voluntarily screen their vegetables for nitrates to ensure the supply is safe. If you are feeding any of these higher-risk vegetables to an infant under six months, it is safest to purchase commercially prepared and screened infant food. Infants over six months should be able to tolerate the nitrates that might be in these vegetables.

Food Safety

In the first few months of your baby's life, it is important to sterilize items that may come in contact with her in order to minimize her exposure to bacteria and viruses. However, once your baby is a little mobile and begins to explore the world with her mouth, it is not necessary to sterilize everything in her environment except bottles and nipples.

The most important way to decrease the risk of a food-borne illness is to follow safe food-handling practices. Safe food-handling practices for infants and children are no different than for adults. Hand washing is the first step to every adventure in the kitchen.

Here are some quick tips for food safety from the United States Department of Agriculture Food Safety and Inspection Service:

- Frequently clean the areas where you prepare food.
- Separate meat and poultry from other foods; do not cross-contaminate.
- Always cook food to proper temperatures.
- Refrigerate your food right away so bacteria cannot grow on it.

Cooking and preparing food safely involves following guidelines that help decrease the chance that bacteria can grow in your food. These recommendations help ensure that your baby will not get food poisoning due to unsafe kitchen practices.

Once you purchase or cook your food, you need to safely store it. The rule is to always put perishable food in the refrigerator within two hours. If you live in a hot climate or the temperature is over 90 degrees, that time decreases to only one hour. Cook or freeze chicken, fish, or ground meat within two days. If it is heartier meat like beef, veal, lamb, or pork you can wait three to five days before freezing. Store your uncooked poultry, fish, or meat separately from fruit, vegetables, or any other raw food to help stop cross-contamination. Refrigerators should be at 40°F or below, and freezers should be at 0°F.

In food preparation, use separate cutting boards for raw meats so that they won't contaminate the fruits and vegetables that you are preparing. Wash cutting boards thoroughly in hot, soapy water after each use. There are three ways to thaw frozen meats. You can place them in the refrigerator to thaw; you can submerge the meats in cold water in the sink and change the water every thirty minutes; or you can use the microwave to thaw frozen items. It is not safe to thaw foods on the counter at room temperature. Letting meat sit out at room temperature allows bacteria to grow on the food.

Once food is thawed, it is possible to refreeze it without cooking it first, but only if you thawed it in the refrigerator. If you thaw it in the microwave or in cold water, cook the food and then refreeze it. It is recommended that you go through this cycle only once and not continue to freeze and thaw the same food over and over again.

When cooking foods, make sure that you cook meats to the proper temperature. Use a meat thermometer to tell if the food has reached the proper temperature. Beef, veal, lamb, roasts, and chops all need to reach 145°F. Pork and ground meat (beef, veal, and lamb) need to reach 160°F. Poultry, such as chicken and turkey, needs to reach 165°F.

Kitchen Equipment, Tools, and Gadgets

If you go into any kitchen supply store you will find a gadget for everything. This can be overwhelming; however, you do not have to buy all these gadgets to be a successful cook. Do you need fancy equipment to make your own baby food and cook healthy organic food for your family? No! Most people have everything that they need to get started making their own organic baby food. Here is a list of some of the basics to make sure you have on hand:

- **Food processor or blender:** The size of the processor or blender needed depends on how much puréeing you want to do at one time. If you are planning to prepare large batches of purées at one time, a large processor will be helpful. Most people will be successful with puréeing in a simple blender or mini processor.
- **Sieve or strainer:** Your pasta colander is not sufficient for straining purées for your infant. A small metal strainer is needed to catch the fine seeds and fibers that did not get puréed fine enough. Make sure that this item is in good condition with no rust on the strainer.

- **Steamer:** A small metal collapsible steamer that fits inside your saucepan is fine for steaming small batches. If you plan on steaming large batches, you might want to invest in a combined rice and vegetable steamer. This is a nice addition to your kitchen for more than just purées. You can continue to use this to cook rice and steam vegetables perfectly without having to watch the stove constantly.
- **Ice cube trays or small glass containers:** This is the easiest way to store your prepared purées. Once your foods are puréed, you can pour them into ice cube trays and freeze. Once frozen, pop them out and into storage containers for your freezer. Each ice cube–sized portion is about a 2-tablespoon portion of baby food, or about 1 ounce. As your child gets older, it is helpful to use small glass containers for freezing larger portions. Then these containers can go right from the freezer to the microwave. Label and date your containers so you know how long the purées have been in storage.
- **Appliances:** A microwave is wonderful for thawing or heating up purées and toddler meals for your child. Make sure to always microwave in glass containers or on plates. Microwaving in plastics can make the plastics unstable and may not be healthy for your family in the long term. Microwaves often heat foods unevenly, so be sure to test the temperature of the food. There could be very hot spots in the food that can burn your baby. Stir food well after heating and always test the temperature before feeding your baby.
- **Handy helpers:** Some items to keep handy in your kitchen drawers that are helpful for making organic foods for your child include the following: vegetable peeler, assortment of different-sized knifes, wet and dry measuring cups, measuring spoons, kitchen timer, spatula, whisk, kitchen scissors, small hand grater, meat thermometer, and wooden spoons.
- **Feeding supplies:** A small bowl, a few shallow plastic spoons, and a bib are all that you need to start. Be sure to

test the temperature of the food yourself. Do not rely on the spoons and bowls that change color if the food is too hot.

- **High chair:** Your baby should be able to sit in the high chair to start taking some of his first solids. Initially, it might make your child more comfortable with this new experience for you to hold him. Be careful not to continue this past the first couple of feeds. You want your child to learn that eating is done in the high chair. This helps establish a regular eating pattern with your child from the beginning.

As you can see, a few small investments are all that you need to begin cooking and preparing healthful organic food for your baby and family. Organizing and equipping your kitchen is fun way to start off this adventure in organic cooking!

The Organic Family Pantry

If you are new to organic cooking, choosing and purchasing organic products for your kitchen can be overwhelming. Restocking your kitchen pantry can be a fun way to jump-start your family on the path to organic eating. Here is a list of some common organic ingredients that are used in this cookbook; having these items on hand will make sure that you are prepared. With a well-stocked pantry and some good recipe ideas, you will always be able to answer the question "What's for dinner?"

Staples in an Organic Family Pantry

BAKING GOODS
- Whole-wheat pastry flour
- All-purpose flour
- Brown sugar
- Baking powder
- Baking salt

- Old-fashioned oats
- Cornstarch
- White whole-wheat flour

BREADS/CEREALS
- Whole-wheat bread
- Whole-wheat tortillas
- Corn tortillas
- Whole-wheat cereal
- Whole-wheat English muffins
- Whole-wheat pizza crust
- Whole-wheat croutons
- Whole-wheat pasta

CANNED GOODS
- Beans: black, pinto, cannellini, kidney
- Diced tomatoes
- Sunflower nut butter
- Pineapple
- Pumpkin
- Light coconut milk
- Marinara sauce
- Applesauce

DAIRY PRODUCTS
- Milk
- Sour cream
- Greek yogurt
- Shredded cheese
- Cream cheese
- Omega-3–fortified eggs
- Butter

FROZEN FOODS

- Berries
- Mangos
- Spinach
- Broccoli
- Mixed vegetables
- Chicken breasts
- Fish portions
- Apple juice concentrate

GRAINS AND DRIED BEANS

- Brown rice
- Arborio rice
- Barley
- Quinoa
- Oatmeal
- Kasha
- Grits
- Lentils
- Black beans
- Pinto beans
- Wheat germ
- Flaxseed meal
- Whole flaxseed

OILS, SAUCES, AND SEASONINGS

- Olive oil
- Canola oil
- Vegetable bouillon
- Chicken bouillon
- Chicken broth
- Beef broth
- Barbecue sauce
- Light agave nectar

- Rice wine vinegar
- Red wine vinegar
- White wine vinegar
- Dijon mustard
- Vegenaise
- Pure maple syrup

PRODUCE
- In-season fresh produce
- Onions
- Garlic
- Avocado
- Banana
- Dried blueberries
- Lemons
- Limes

Take your time shopping when you are new to cooking. Stroll the store aisles, read the labels, and talk to the farmers at the market. You can learn so many tips and tricks by spending time with people who enjoy cooking with organic foods. You will see new and exciting foods each time you go organic grocery shopping. New foods help add variety to your family's meals. Variety in your diet helps you stay adventurous and healthy.

CHAPTER 3

Four to Six Months

Baby's First Rice Cereal

Your baby should only receive rice cereal from a spoon. Do not put rice cereal in your child's bottle.

INGREDIENTS | YIELDS 5–6 TABLESPOONS

1 tablespoon iron-fortified prepared rice cereal
4–5 tablespoons breast milk or formula

Mix all ingredients together. Consistency should be equal to or only slightly thicker than breast milk or formula.

First Taste—Get Your Camera!

Your baby's first taste of infant rice cereal may be more exciting for you than for her! She may make funny faces, be disinterested, or dribble it all over herself. Or, she may look at you like you have been holding out on her and gobble it all up. Enjoy this moment and each opportunity you have to feed your child. They are a gift.

Sweet Pea Purée

Sweet peas are often a child's first vegetable. If he does not like the first taste, continue to offer this periodically. It can take many tries for a child to accept new foods!

INGREDIENTS | YIELDS 1 CUP

1 cup sweet peas
1–2 tablespoons water

1. Steam the peas in the water. Save water when done steaming.

2. Put peas in food processor or blender. Process on and off until desired consistency reached (for ages 4–6 months, consistency should be equal to or only slightly thicker than breast milk or formula). Use a small amount of the cooking liquid to thin the final product if necessary. Work the pulp through a strong strainer to remove any fibrous material.

Freezing Tips

If you are planning on making a large batch of vegetables to freeze, use water to thin out the purée, if needed. Breast milk and formula do not freeze well in purées.

Green Bean Purée

Snap the beans! Remove both ends of the beans by either snapping them off or cutting them with a knife or kitchen scissors.

INGREDIENTS | YIELDS 1 CUP

1 cup green beans
1–2 tablespoons water

1. Steam the green beans in the water. Save water when done steaming.

2. Put beans in food processor or blender. Process on and off until desired consistency reached (for ages 4–6 months, consistency should be equal to or only slightly thicker than breast milk or formula). Use a small amount of the cooking liquid to thin the final product if necessary. If you plan to freeze the final product, do not thin with breast milk or formula. Work the pulp through a strong strainer to remove fibrous materials.

Snapping the Beans

Snapping the beans is an easy way to engage your older children in preparing foods and they will be more likely to accept the dish.

Squash Purée

Most babies love the sweet, smooth consistency of puréed squash.
Acorn and butternut are two of the main varieties.

INGREDIENTS | YIELDS 1 CUP

½ pound squash (variety of your choice)
½ cup water

1. Peel, seed, and chop squash. Steam in steamer with water for 7–10 minutes.
2. Put squash in food processor or blender. Process on and off until desired consistency reached. Use a small amount of the cooking liquid to thin the final product if necessary. If you plan to freeze the final product, do not thin with breast milk or formula. Work the pulp through a strong strainer to remove any fibrous materials.

Sweet Pea and Mango Purée

Frozen organic sweet peas are readily
available and relatively inexpensive.

INGREDIENTS | YIELDS ¼ CUP

2 tablespoons Sweet Pea Purée (see recipe in this chapter)
2 tablespoons Mango Purée (see recipe in this chapter)

In a small bowl, combine all ingredients.

Sweet Potato Purée

Sweet potatoes are easy for most babies to digest, and are a favorite first food. They are also easy to keep on hand, because they last longer than fruit and other vegetables.

INGREDIENTS | YIELDS ¾ CUP

1 medium sweet potato
3 cups of water

1. Peel and chop potato into small pieces that are all about the same size. In a medium-sized pan, bring water to a boil. Place potato in water. Cover and cook for about 10 minutes, until tender. Drain.

2. Place potato in a food processor or blender. Process on and off until desired consistency reached. Use a small amount of the cooking liquid to thin the final product if necessary. If you plan to freeze the final product, do not thin with breast milk or formula.

Apple Purée

Red Delicious, Braeburn, and Gala apples make particularly good apple purée, though almost any variety can be used.

INGREDIENTS | YIELDS ¾ CUP

2 medium apples (variety of your choice)
1–2 tablespoons water

1. Peel and chop apples into small pieces that are all about the same size. In a medium-sized pan, combine the fruit and water. Cover and cook for about 10 minutes until tender.

2. In food processor or blender, combine all ingredients. Process on and off until desired consistency is reached. If you plan to freeze the final product, do not thin with breast milk or formula.

Apple Pops

Freeze your purées in ice cube trays. Put the purée in ice cube trays and cover with plastic wrap and freeze. Pop out a cube when you are ready to use! Each cube is about 2 tablespoons of food.

Avocado Mash

Avocado is a great first food. It's loaded with monounsaturated fat (the good fat), folate, potassium, and fiber. Avocados do have more calories than other fruits and vegetables, so use in moderation.

INGREDIENTS | YIELDS 6 TABLESPOONS

1 medium ripe avocado

1. Slice avocado around the outside lengthwise. Twist both sides off the seed of the avocado. Scoop out flesh from one side of the avocado. Mash until desired consistency is reached.
2. Wrap remaining avocado with the seed in it with plastic wrap and store in the refrigerator.

Can You Freeze an Avocado?

Avocados do not freeze well due to their consistency. You can use lemon juice on the avocado to help prevent browning; however, your baby is not ready for citrus until closer to one year old, so only cut the amount of avocado that you can use in that day. Or, make the family guacamole and pull some plain avocado out for your baby.

Banana Mash

Banana mash does not freeze well so only prepare the amount that you can use for 1–2 feedings. Bananas are an excellent source of potassium.

INGREDIENTS | YIELDS 6 TABLESPOONS

½ ripe banana

1. Peel the banana half, removing any strings.
2. Place banana flesh in bowl.
3. Mash with a fork until desired consistency is reached.

The Perfect Food

Bananas are often called the perfect food. Bananas are an excellent source of potassium, which is helpful for controlling blood pressure. In addition, each banana contains 4 grams of fiber and 2 grams of protein.

Pear Purée

Pears are very sweet, and most babies like them right away. Look for a ripe pear with a good fragrance that yields just slightly to the touch.

INGREDIENTS | YIELDS ¾ CUP

2 medium pears
1–2 tablespoons water

1. Peel, core, and chop the pears into small pieces that are all about the same size.

2. In a medium-sized pan, combine the fruit and water.

3. Cover and cook for about 4–6 minutes, until tender.

4. Place the cooked mixture into a food processor or blender. Process on and off until desired consistency is reached. If you plan to freeze the final product, do not thin with breast milk or formula.

Dried Plum Purée

It is possible to also use whole fresh plums to make a purée. Follow the recipe for Peach Purée found in this chapter, but substitute plums. They may need additional straining due to their fibrous skin!

INGREDIENTS | YIELDS ½ CUP

⅔ cup (4 ounces) pitted dried plums or prunes
3 tablespoons water

1. In food processor or blender, combine plums (or prunes) and water.
2. Process on and off until desired consistency is reached. If the mixture is still too coarse, pass it through a fine strainer.

Regular Old Prunes

Prunes contain 2 grams of fiber per ounce. Your child needs fiber to help maintain a healthy gastrointestinal tract and regular bowel movements. Adding prunes to your child's diet can help keep him regular.

Papaya Purée

Papaya is a fruit that does not freeze well. It is recommended to only make what you can use fresh. It does keep for a few days nicely in the fridge and continues to soften over time.

INGREDIENTS | YIELDS ¾ CUP

½ medium papaya, cut lengthwise
1–2 tablespoons formula or breast milk

1. Scrape the seeds out of the papaya and discard them.
2. Scoop out the flesh of the papaya and put in bowl.
3. Add formula or breast milk to papaya and mash with fork.
4. Mash until desired consistency reached.

How Do You Know If a Papaya Is Ripe?

You want to buy a papaya when it is almost ripe and is half-green and half-yellow. It will take two to four days to ripen from this stage. You can begin to smell the papaya as it ripens, and you can tell it's ripe when it is slightly sensitive to pressure.

Peach Purée

If peaches are not in season, buy frozen unsweetened peaches, thaw, and use to purée for your baby.

INGREDIENTS | YIELDS ¾ CUP

2 medium peaches
1–2 tablespoons water

1. Cut peaches in half lengthwise and twist off of pit.
2. In food processor or blender, combine peaches and water. Process on and off until desired consistency is reached.

Apricot Purée

If fresh apricots are not available, buy dried apricots. Simmer the dried apricots on the stove in water for about 8–10 minutes until tender and then purée.

INGREDIENTS | YIELDS ¾ CUP

4 medium apricots
1–2 tablespoons water

1. Cut apricots in half lengthwise and twist off of pit.
2. In food processor or blender, combine apricots and water. Process on and off until desired consistency is reached. Work the pulp through a strong strainer to remove any fibrous materials.

Move Over, Carrots

Carrots are not the only foods that are an excellent source of vitamin A! Apricots are excellent sources of vitamin A, beta carotene, lycopene, and fiber. Vitamin A, beta carotene, and lycopene all help protect eye function and are great sources of antioxidants. The fiber in apricots is good for your cholesterol level and can help maintain regularity.

Mango Purée

Frozen mango slices can also work as a purée. Just thaw the slices and then purée according to the following directions.

INGREDIENTS | YIELDS ¾ CUP

2 medium mangos
1–2 tablespoons water

1. Remove flesh from mangos.
2. In food processor or blender, combine mangos and water. Process on and off until desired consistency is reached. Work the pulp through a strong strainer to remove any fibrous materials.

How Do You Cut a Mango?

There are two flat sides to a mango and a large square pit in the middle. Cut off the two flat sides. Take a knife and make lengthwise and crosswise scores in the mango but do not cut through the skin. Take your thumbs and turn this "inside out." Slice the mango pieces off the skin. Repeat around the whole mango.

Pumpkin Pear Rice Cereal

*Use whatever variety of pear is fresh
at your grocery store or farmers' market for this dish.
Good choices include Bartlett, Anjou, and Bosc.*

INGREDIENTS | YIELDS 6 TABLESPOONS

2 tablespoons prepared iron-fortified rice cereal (with either breast milk or formula)
2 tablespoons Pumpkin Purée (see recipe in this chapter)
2 tablespoons Pear Purée (see recipe in this chapter)

Combine all ingredients in a small bowl.

Green Beans and Rice Cereal

*This is a traditional baby-food combination and
a great way for your baby to get her veggies.*

INGREDIENTS | YIELDS ¼ CUP

2 tablespoons prepared iron-fortified rice cereal (with either breast milk
or formula)
2 tablespoons Green Bean Purée (see recipe in this chapter)

In a small bowl, add the ingredients and mix well to combine.

Mango, Peach, and Rice Cereal

These two fruits complement each other with their sweet tanginess.

INGREDIENTS | YIELDS 6 TABLESPOONS

2 tablespoons prepared iron-fortified rice cereal (with either breast milk
or formula)
2 tablespoons Mango Purée (see recipe in this chapter)
2 tablespoons Peach Purée (see recipe in this chapter)

In a small bowl, combine all ingredients.

Green Beans, Mango, and Rice Cereal

Although to adults this combination might seem unconventional, babies are just learning about different food tastes and textures. Babies should not be limited by an adult palate.

INGREDIENTS | YIELDS 6 TABLESPOONS

2 tablespoons prepared iron-fortified rice cereal (with either breast milk or formula)

2 tablespoons Green Bean Purée (see recipe in this chapter)

2 tablespoons Mango Purée (see recipe in this chapter)

In a small bowl, combine all ingredients.

Hot-Blooded Mangos

Since mango trees cannot tolerate cool weather, they are not locally available in many parts of the United States. However, frozen organic mango is available in many well-stocked supermarkets.

Banana, Sweet Pea, and Rice Cereal

If your child doesn't like sweet peas on their own, this combination might do the trick.

INGREDIENTS | YIELDS 6 TABLESPOONS

2 tablespoons prepared iron-fortified rice cereal (with either breast milk or formula)

2 tablespoons Banana Mash (see recipe in this chapter)

2 tablespoons Sweet Pea Purée (see recipe in this chapter)

In a small bowl add all the ingredients and mix well to combine.

Banana and Oatmeal Cereal

Remember that bananas tend to constipate babies, so use this recipe only occasionally.

INGREDIENTS | YIELDS ¼ CUP

2 tablespoons prepared iron-fortified oatmeal cereal (with either breast milk or formula)

2 tablespoons Banana Mash (see recipe in this chapter)

In a small bowl, combine all ingredients.

Papaya, Pear, and Oatmeal Cereal

Jarred pear sauce can be used in place of the Pear Purée.

INGREDIENTS | YIELDS 6 TABLESPOONS

2 tablespoons prepared iron-fortified oatmeal cereal (with either breast milk or formula)

2 tablespoons Papaya Purée (see recipe in this chapter)

2 tablespoons Pear Purée (see recipe in this chapter)

In a small bowl add all the ingredients and mix well to combine.

Banana, Apricot, and Oatmeal Cereal

This combination includes lots of nutrients that a growing baby needs, including potassium, iron, and vitamin A.

INGREDIENTS | YIELDS 6 TABLESPOONS

2 tablespoons prepared iron-fortified oatmeal cereal (with either breast milk or formula)
2 tablespoons Banana Mash (see recipe in this chapter)
2 tablespoons Apricot Purée (see recipe in this chapter)

In a small bowl, combine all ingredients.

Apple and Oatmeal Cereal

This combination is a classic because it is an almost universal baby-pleaser.

INGREDIENTS | YIELDS ¼ CUP

2 tablespoons prepared iron-fortified oatmeal cereal (with either breast milk or formula)
2 tablespoons Apple Purée (see recipe in this chapter)

In a small bowl, combine all ingredients.

Apples, the Local Option
Although crabapples are the only apple that is native to North America, apples today are grown in all fifty states. Look for locally grown organic apples at the farmers' market in the fall.

Pumpkin, Peach, and Oatmeal Cereal

The combination of pumpkin and peach will result in a vibrant orange color.

INGREDIENTS | YIELDS 6 TABLESPOONS

2 tablespoons prepared iron-fortified oatmeal cereal (with either breast milk or formula)

2 tablespoons Pumpkin Purée (see recipe in this chapter)

2 tablespoons Peach Purée (see recipe in this chapter)

Combine all ingredients.

Papaya, Apple, and Oatmeal Cereal

This combination is a sweet and yummy way to start the day.

INGREDIENTS | YIELDS 6 TABLESPOONS

2 tablespoons prepared iron-fortified oatmeal cereal (with either breast milk or formula)

2 tablespoons Papaya Purée (see recipe in this chapter)

2 tablespoons Apple Purée (see recipe in this chapter)

In a small bowl, combine all ingredients.

Amazing Apple Juice

Between 20,000 and 40,000 tons of apples are converted into apple juice every year. Due to the demand for organics, the share of organic apple juice is steadily increasing. Although apples are converted to juice only during the fall (typically in October), thanks to sterile storing and packaging, apple juice can be enjoyed throughout the year.

Avocado and Barley Cereal

When making a salad for the whole family, set aside some of the
avocado and mash it up for the youngest family member.

INGREDIENTS | YIELDS ¼ CUP

2 tablespoons prepared iron-fortified barley cereal (with either breast
milk or formula)
2 tablespoons Avocado Mash (see recipe in this chapter)

In a small bowl, combine all ingredients.

Avocados, a Native Fruit

Avocados are native to North America, originating in Central America
and Mexico thousands of years ago. Today, more than 90 percent of
the avocados at the supermarket come from California.

Dried Plum and Barley Cereal

The same process used to make the Dried Plum Purée can be used
to turn dried apricots into an apricot purée.

INGREDIENTS | YIELDS ¼ CUP

2 tablespoons prepared iron-fortified barley cereal (with either breast
milk or formula)
2 tablespoons Dried Plum Purée (see recipe in this chapter)

Add all the ingredients to a small bowl and mix well to
combine.

Apricot, Dried Plum, and Barley Cereal

This dish is the perfect choice for a constipated baby.

INGREDIENTS | YIELDS 6 TABLESPOONS

2 tablespoons prepared iron-fortified barley cereal (with either breast milk or formula)

2 tablespoons Apricot Purée (see recipe in this chapter)

2 tablespoons Dried Plum Purée (see recipe in this chapter)

In a small bowl, combine all ingredients.

Yummy Cousins

Apricots and plums are part of the same family "tree." Both are part of the plant family genus *Plumus*. Like their cousin, apricots are delicious fresh, but they are also nutritious and delicious when dried.

Apple, Pumpkin, and Barley Cereal

Pumpkin Purée adds a creamy texture to this combination.

INGREDIENTS | YIELDS 6 TABLESPOONS

2 tablespoons prepared iron-fortified barley cereal (with either breast milk or formula)

2 tablespoons Apple Purée (see recipe in this chapter)

2 tablespoons Pumpkin Purée (see recipe in this chapter)

Combine all ingredients in a small bowl.

Organic Jarred Applesauce

Organic applesauce is readily available. Keep a jar or two on hand for days when life gets in the way of cooking. It can be combined with cereal and breast milk or formula, mixed with a vegetable purée or just served on its own. Most commercially available brands have a very smooth consistency that works well with even beginning eaters. Remember to make sure that there is no added sugar. If the texture is lumpy, you should still purée it for baby.

Avocado Banana Mash

These two buttery items make such a great combination for your baby. Both have similar textures and blend together nicely!

INGREDIENTS | YIELDS ¼ CUP

2 tablespoons Avocado Mash (see recipe in this chapter)
2 tablespoons Banana Mash (see recipe in this chapter)

Combine all ingredients in a small bowl and mash with a fork until desired consistency.

Bananas Not Ripe?

If your bananas are not quite ripe, heat them in the microwave for a few seconds to soften to the correct consistency for mashing. Another way to ripen bananas is to place them in a brown bag. This will speed up the process.

Pear Mango Purée

Cantaloupe can also be used as a substitute for either of these ingredients and makes a nice purée as well. All these orange fruits together help provide your baby with vitamin A.

INGREDIENTS | YIELDS ¼ CUP

2 tablespoons Pear Purée (see recipe in this chapter)
2 tablespoons Mango Purée (see recipe in this chapter)

In a small bowl, combine all ingredients.

Papaya and Banana Mash

A nickname for the papaya is the "tree melon."

INGREDIENTS | YIELDS ¼ CUP

2 tablespoons Papaya Purée (see recipe in this chapter)
2 tablespoons Banana Mash (see recipe in this chapter)

In a small bowl, combine all ingredients and mix well.

Apricot Pear Purée

There are 6 grams of fiber in a medium pear! These can be used as well as prunes to help with your baby's stool pattern.

INGREDIENTS | YIELDS ¼ CUP

2 tablespoons Apricot Purée (see recipe in this chapter)
2 tablespoons Pear Purée (see recipe in this chapter)

In a small bowl, combine all ingredients.

Sweet Pea and Apple Purée

If your baby did not like plain sweet peas, try this mixture with apples. The sweet taste of the apples may help your baby to accept the peas in disguise.

INGREDIENTS | YIELDS ¼ CUP

2 tablespoons Sweet Pea Purée (see recipe in this chapter)
2 tablespoons Apple Purée (see recipe in this chapter)

In a small bowl, combine all ingredients.

Are Peas a Vegetable?
You may be surprised to learn that peas are a legume or bean. A legume is a plant that bears fruits in the form of pods. These pods grow and then hold the seeds that we know as peas or beans.

Peach and Avocado Mash

In the summer, many local nurseries allow you to go and pick your own peaches. Make this a fun family activity with your children as they grow.

INGREDIENTS | YIELDS ¼ CUP

2 tablespoons Peach Purée (see recipe in this chapter)
2 tablespoons Avocado Mash (see recipe in this chapter)

In a small bowl, combine all ingredients and mash with a fork until desired consistency.

Mango and Apricot Purée

Once you try a fruit or vegetable and your child has no reaction after four to seven days, try combining different items for new flavors.

INGREDIENTS | YIELDS ¼ CUP

2 tablespoons Mango Purée (see recipe in this chapter)
2 tablespoons Apricot Purée (see recipe in this chapter)

In a small bowl, combine all ingredients.

Are Unusual Combinations Okay?
Babies are developing their taste buds. Try unusual combinations of fruits and vegetables, even if they sound strange to you. Your child may love a combination of plums and sweet peas even if it does not sound good to you. Experiment and have fun with feeding your child.

Avocado Pumpkin Mash

The color of this combination might not be appealing to an adult, but this won't be a problem for your baby.

INGREDIENTS | YIELDS ¼ CUP

2 tablespoons Avocado Mash (see recipe in this chapter)
2 tablespoons Pumpkin Purée (see recipe in this chapter)

In a small bowl, combine all ingredients.

Dried Plum and Pear Purée

*You can use fresh plums in season in place of
dried plums in this yummy purée.*

INGREDIENTS | YIELDS ¼ CUP

2 tablespoons Dried Plum Purée (see recipe in this chapter)
2 tablespoons Pear Purée (see recipe in this chapter)

In a small bowl, combine all ingredients and mix well.

Peach Pear Purée

*Different varieties of pears are available all throughout the year,
so experiment with all the taste variations.*

INGREDIENTS | YIELDS ¼ CUP

2 tablespoons Peach Purée (see recipe in this chapter)
2 tablespoons Pear Purée (see recipe in this chapter)

In a small bowl, combine all ingredients.

Baked Pears

Another delicious way to enjoy fresh pears is to bake them. First preheat oven to 350°F. Then cut pears into chunks. Cover and bake for
40–60 minutes. Purée baby's portion, and serve the larger chunks to
the rest of the family.

Banana Pumpkin Mash

Mix this purée with 1 teaspoon sunflower seed butter for a yummy spread for toast or muffins when your baby is a little older.

INGREDIENTS | YIELDS ¼ CUP

2 tablespoons Banana Mash (see recipe in this chapter)
2 tablespoons Pumpkin Purée (see recipe in this chapter)

In a small bowl, combine all ingredients.

Sunflower Seed Butter

Since peanut butter is off-limits due to potential food allergies for little children, sunflower seed butter steps in to create delicious recipes. Due to its peanut-butter–like consistency, it shouldn't be given to children under three years on its own, but it can be baked up in muffins or blended in smoothies and dips. Sunflower seed butter is available commercially or you can make your own by tossing roasted sunflower seeds (without the shells) in the food processor with a little canola oil. Process until smooth.

Green Beans and Avocado Mash

Green beans are loaded with vitamins and minerals, including K, C, potassium, and iron.

INGREDIENTS | YIELDS ¼ CUP

2 tablespoons Green Bean Purée (see recipe in this chapter)
2 tablespoons Avocado Mash (see recipe in this chapter)

Combine all ingredients in a small bowl.

Pumpkin Purée

For a shortcut, use a can of plain, organic pumpkin—just open the can and serve. Make sure to buy plain pumpkin with no added spices, sugars, or dairy products.

INGREDIENTS | YIELDS 1 CUP

½ small pumpkin (approximately ½ pound)
½ cup water

1. Peel, seed, and chop pumpkin. Steam in steamer with water for 7–10 minutes.

2. Put pumpkin in food processor or blender. Process on and off until desired consistency reached. Use a small amount of the cooking water to thin the final product if necessary. If you plan to freeze the final product, do not thin with breast milk or formula. Work the pulp through a strong strainer to remove any fibrous materials.

Pumpkins Are Not Just for Halloween

Choose a "pie pumpkin" to make this purée. Wash the outside of the pumpkin, cut in half, and scrape out the seeds. Remove the stem, put in microwaveable bowl and add 2"–3" of water, and cover. Cook on high for 15 minutes and check to see if the pumpkin is tender. Cook another 15 minutes on high until done. The pumpkin is done when it is tender enough to scrape out with a fork. Scrape flesh out and purée.

CHAPTER 4

Six to Nine Months

Brown Rice

Brown rice is a tender, delicious whole grain.

INGREDIENTS | YIELDS 2 CUPS

1 cup brown rice
2 cups water

1. Combine brown rice and water in a small saucepan. Bring to a boil.
2. Cover, reduce heat, and simmer for 40 minutes or until water is absorbed.
3. Remove saucepan from heat, and let sit covered for 5 minutes.
4. Fluff with a fork and serve.

Basic Barley

Barley is an easy and delicious grain that is as versatile as rice.

INGREDIENTS | YIELDS 3½ CUPS

1 cup pearl barley
3 cups water

1. In a small saucepan, combine barley and water. Cover saucepan.
2. Simmer for 45–55 minutes, or until barley is tender.

Quinoa

Not only is quinoa high in protein, but it is also high in fiber and essential amino acids. Make sure your child tolerates rice, oatmeal, and barley before introducing quinoa.

INGREDIENTS | YIELDS 2 CUPS

1 cup quinoa
2 cups water

1. Thoroughly rinse quinoa under running water.
2. Combine quinoa and the water in a medium saucepan.
3. Bring to a boil.
4. Reduce heat, cover, and simmer for 15 minutes or until the outer ring of each grain separates.
5. Fluff with a fork before serving.

Oatmeal

Oatmeal is a high-protein, high-fiber whole grain, and it's delicious to boot!

INGREDIENTS | YIELDS 2 CUPS

2 cups water
1 cup old-fashioned rolled oats

1. In a medium saucepan, bring water to a boil.
2. Add oatmeal, reduce heat, and simmer, stirring occasionally, for 5–10 minutes or until water is absorbed and oats are tender.

Kasha (Roasted Buckwheat)

Kasha, most often found in Eastern European cooking, is a nutty grain with a fluffy texture.

INGREDIENTS | YIELDS 2 CUPS

2 cups water
1 tablespoon olive oil
1 cup kasha

1. In a medium saucepan, bring water and olive oil to a boil.
2. Add kasha, cover, and reduce heat. Simmer for 10 minutes. Fluff before serving.

Eastern European Comfort Food

Kasha, or roasted buckwheat, is a common breakfast food throughout Eastern Europe. Buckwheat, which is not related to wheat, is also commonly found a flour that is used in pancakes and other baked goods. Because it is a good source of protein, fiber, magnesium, and manganese, it is a good addition a well-stocked pantry.

Basic Grits

Grits are a good source of dietary fiber.

INGREDIENTS | YIELDS 1 CUP

¼ cup grits
1 cup water

1. In a small saucepan, combine grits and water.
2. Bring to a boil, stirring constantly.
3. Reduce heat, cover, and simmer for 5 minutes.

Lentils

Lentils feature prominently in cuisines from around the world, including the Middle East and India. If your baby needs a smoother texture, purée lentils before serving.

INGREDIENTS | YIELDS 2 CUPS

1 cup dried lentils
4 cups water

1. Rinse lentils under running water, and pick over to remove any stones or debris.

2. Combine lentils and water in medium saucepan and simmer gently with lid tilted for 30–45 minutes, or until lentils are tender.

3. Drain off excess water before serving.

Split Peas

Split peas are a great source of protein, fiber, and iron. If your baby needs a smoother texture, purée split peas before serving.

INGREDIENTS | YIELDS 2 CUPS

1 cup dried green split peas
2 cups water

1. Rinse split peas under running water, and pick over to remove any stones or debris.
2. Combine split peas and water in a small saucepan. Bring to a boil.
3. Reduce heat, cover, and simmer for 30–45 minutes.
4. Drain off extra water before serving.

Green or Yellow?

Split peas come in green and yellow. They can be used interchangeably, as they both cook up tender and are great sources of protein and iron.

Black Bean Mash

Dried beans are extremely affordable, where canned beans are extremely convenient. Either option would work for this recipe.

INGREDIENTS | YIELDS 2 CUPS

1 cup dried black beans (or 1 [15-ounce] can of black beans)
4 cups water
1 tablespoon olive oil

1. Soak dried beans in water for 6–8 hours or overnight before cooking. Drain soaking water from beans and rinse.

2. In a medium saucepan combine soaked beans with 4 cups water, and bring to a simmer with the lid tilted. Cook 1–1½ hours or until tender. Drain and rinse cooked beans (or drain and rinse canned beans, if using).

3. In a medium saucepan or sauté pan, heat olive oil over medium heat. Add beans and heat through for 1–2 minutes, or until desired temperature is reached.

4. Remove from heat and mash beans with a potato masher or fork.

Refried Pinto Beans

This is a mild version of a classic Mexican dish.

INGREDIENTS | YIELDS 2 CUPS

1 cup dried pinto beans (or 1 [15-ounce] can)
4 cups water
1 tablespoon olive oil
½ medium sweet onion, finely chopped
1 clove garlic, minced
1 teaspoon ground cumin

1. Soak dried beans in water for 6–8 hours or overnight before cooking. Drain soaking water from beans, and rinse.

2. In a medium saucepan, combine soaked beans with water, and bring to a simmer with lid tilted. Cook 1–1½ hours or until tender. Drain and rinse either cooked beans or canned beans, if using.

3. In a medium saucepan or sauté pan, heat olive oil over medium heat. Add onion and garlic. Cook until onion is tender, 3–5 minutes. Add cooked beans and cumin, and heat through for 1–2 minutes, or until desired temperature is reached.

4. Remove from heat, and mash with a potato masher or fork.

Apple and Pear Purée

For this recipe or other recipes that call for a sweeter pear, try a red Bartlett, Comice, or forelle type.

INGREDIENTS | YIELDS ¼ CUP

2 tablespoons Apple Purée (see Chapter 3)
2 tablespoons Pear Purée (see Chapter 3)

In a small bowl, combine all ingredients.

Apricot, Pear, and Barley Cereal

This fiber-rich cereal is also a good source of vitamins A and C.

INGREDIENTS | YIELDS 6 TABLESPOONS

2 tablespoons iron-fortified barley cereal (prepared with breast milk or formula)
2 tablespoons Apricot Purée (see Chapter 3)
2 tablespoons Pear Purée (see Chapter 3)

In a small bowl, combine all the ingredients.

Apple, Sweet Potato, and Cinnamon Purée

As your baby gets older, you can begin to experiment with slightly thicker mashes and adding spices. If your baby has trouble with the thickness, add more apple purée to thin. Try the thicker mash again in a week or two.

INGREDIENTS | YIELDS 6 TABLESPOONS

2 tablespoons Apple Purée (see Chapter 3)
¼ cup Sweet Potato Purée (see Chapter 3)
⅛ teaspoon ground cinnamon

In a small bowl, combine all the ingredients and mix well.

Banana and Blueberry Purée

Be sure that your baby is wearing a bib for this one—blueberries stain!

INGREDIENTS | YIELDS 1½ CUPS

1 ripe medium banana
½ cup fresh or frozen blueberries
2 tablespoons water

1. Purée the banana and blueberries in blender or food processor.
2. Add water and blend to reach desired consistency.

Butternut Squash and Corn Purée

Making a smooth purée is a safe way to serve the delicious taste of sweet corn to your baby.

INGREDIENTS | YIELDS 1½ CUPS

½ cup peeled butternut squash chunks
½ cup water
¼ cup frozen sweet corn

1. In a medium saucepan, combine squash, water, and corn and bring to a boil.
2. Stir while cooking to ensure that squash cooks evenly. Cook until tender, 8–10 minutes.
3. Transfer to a food processor or blender. Purée, using additional water as necessary to achieve age-appropriate consistency.

Fall Harvest Purée

This beta carotene–rich dish highlights some of autumn's best delights.

INGREDIENTS | YIELDS 6 TABLESPOONS

2 tablespoons Apple Purée (see Chapter 3)
2 tablespoons Pumpkin Purée (see Chapter 3)
2 tablespoons Sweet Potato Purée (see Chapter 3)

In a small bowl, combine all ingredients and mix well.

Homemade Applesauce

Make a stockpot full of this delicious sauce during the fall, and freeze in 1–cup containers. It will stay good for up to 6 months in your freezer.

INGREDIENTS | YIELDS 2½ CUPS

3 large sweet apples
⅛ teaspoon ground cinnamon
Enough water to cover apples

1. Peel and core the apples and cut them into chunks.

2. In a large saucepan over medium heat, combine apple chunks and cinnamon. Cover apples with water. Cook until apples are very tender and start to break apart.

3. Mash with a potato masher or the back of a spoon. Transfer to blender or food processor if a finer consistency is needed.

Applesauce for Baking

Many of the recipes for baked goods in this book use applesauce mixed with baking powder. Homemade applesauce is perfect for this. Mash the applesauce to a smooth consistency and then follow the baking recipe directions.

Apple and Carrot Mash

The natural sweetness of carrots is highlighted by the sweet taste of the applesauce in this sunny-colored dish.

INGREDIENTS | YIELDS 1 CUP

1 medium carrot

½ cup Homemade Applesauce (see recipe in this chapter)

1. Peel carrot and cut into small slices or chunks. Steam carrot using either a steamer basket or microwave.

2. Purée carrot in a blender or food processor using reserved steaming water to achieve age-appropriate consistency.

3. Combine carrot and applesauce in a medium bowl, and mix well.

Not So Fast, Honey!

When it's time to start thinking about adding sweeteners to your baby's diet, whether it's for baking or cooking, one natural choice needs to wait. Babies should not have any honey until after one year. Their immature digestive systems cannot adequately process honey, and it can lead to a form of botulism, a serious food poisoning. If you need to turn to a sweetener before one year old, consider apple juice concentrate, maple syrup, or agave nectar.

Mango Banana Purée

One quarter of a banana should yield 2 tablespoons of mashed banana. Transfer the remainder of the banana to a freezer bag and freeze for use in a smoothie.

INGREDIENTS | YIELDS ¼ CUP

2 tablespoons Banana Mash (see Chapter 3)
2 tablespoons Mango Purée (see Chapter 3)

In a small bowl, combine all ingredients.

Two-Potato Mash

Because Yukon gold potatoes are so flavorful, it is the perfect potato to use for this dish, which doesn't contain any added salt.

INGREDIENTS | YIELDS ½ CUP

1 small Yukon gold potato
2 tablespoons water
½ teaspoon canola oil
¼ cup Sweet Potato Purée (see Chapter 3)

1. Wash and peel potato and cut into small chunks.
2. In a small saucepan, bring potato and water to a boil. Cook until tender, about 8–10 minutes.
3. Transfer potato to a food processor or blender with oil. Purée.
4. Add both potato purées to a medium bowl and stir to combine.

Papaya and Banana Mash

You can store a ripe banana in the refrigerator for a few days. The peel will turn brown but the banana flesh will stay yellow.

INGREDIENTS | YIELDS ¼ CUP

2 tablespoons Papaya Purée (see Chapter 3)
2 tablespoons Banana Mash (see Chapter 3)

Combine all ingredients in a small bowl, and mash with a fork until desired consistency.

Can You Freeze Banana Purée?

Bananas are best if mashed fresh. Bananas need lemon juice added to them to prevent browning and young babies should not have citrus until closer to one year of age. If you are making this for an older child, you can add citrus and freeze, but otherwise, mash bananas fresh.

Peach Raspberry Purée

Raspberry bushes grow easily in backyards around the country. Consider planting one for fresh-picked fruit during the summer.

INGREDIENTS | YIELDS ½ CUP

¼ cup raspberries
¼ cup Peach Purée (see Chapter 3)

1. Wash raspberries and drain, but do not dry.
2. Transfer moist raspberries to a food processor or blender and purée.
3. Pass raspberry purée through a fine-meshed sieve or strainer to remove seeds.
4. Combine with Peach Purée in a medium bowl.

Potato and Plum Purée

Different varieties of plums are ripe all throughout the summer, so take advantage of the luscious juiciness of this treat by mixing up some of this sweet and creamy dish.

INGREDIENTS | YIELDS 6 TABLESPOONS

1 small russet potato
2 tablespoons water
1 small, ripe plum

1. Wash and peel potato and cut into small chunks.
2. In a small saucepan, bring potato and water to a boil. Cook until tender, about 8–10 minutes.
3. Peel plum, remove seed, and chop into chunks.
4. Combine fresh plum and cooked potato in food processor or blender. Purée until smooth.

Pumpkin and Parsnip Purée

What to do with parsnips that show up in your box of produce from the farm in early winter? Cook this sweet treat for your baby!

INGREDIENTS | YIELDS ¼ CUP

1 small parsnip
¼ cup Pumpkin Purée (see Chapter 3)

1. Peel parsnip and cut into small slices or chunks.
2. Steam parsnip using either a steamer basket or microwave.
3. Purée parsnip using reserved steaming water to achieve age-appropriate consistency.
4. Combine parsnip purée and Pumpkin Purée in a small bowl.

Spinach and Potato Purée

Fresh spinach holds a lot of dirt and sand. The best way to wash it is to submerge it in a bowl of cold water, drain, and repeat the process until the water remains clear.

INGREDIENTS | YIELDS ½ CUP

1 small russet potato
¼ cup chopped spinach
⅛–¼ cup water

1. Wash, peel, and chop potato into small chunks.
2. In a small saucepan, combine potato, spinach, and water.
3. Bring to a boil, and cook until the potato is tender, approximately 5–10 minutes, depending on the size of the chunks.
4. Transfer potato and spinach to a blender or food processor. Purée until smooth, adding as much reserved cooking water as necessary for age-appropriate consistency.

Rutabaga and Pear Purée

Rutabagas are beta carotene–rich root vegetables that grow best in cold climates, such as the northern United States and Canada.

INGREDIENTS | YIELDS 1 CUP

1 small rutabaga
⅛–¼ cup water
½ cup Pear Purée (see Chapter 3)

1. Peel rutabaga and cut off ends. Cut into chunks.
2. In a small saucepan, combine rutabaga and water. Bring to a boil. Boil until soft, approximately 10 minutes.
3. Transfer rutabaga and reserved cooking water to a food processor or blender. Purée until smooth.
4. In a medium bowl, combine with Pear Purée.

Rutabaga, the Turnip's Cousin
Rutabaga, a sweet, delicious fall root vegetable, is actually a cross between a turnip and a cabbage. Because they're closely related to turnips, rutabagas and turnips can be used interchangeably in recipes.

Sweet Potato and Carrot Purée

*Vitamins A and C team up with a healthy dose
of dietary fiber in this vibrant dish.*

INGREDIENTS | YIELDS ½ CUP

1 medium carrot
¼ cup Sweet Potato Purée (see Chapter 3)

1. Peel carrot and cut into small slices or chunks.

2. Steam carrot using either a steamer basket or microwave.

3. Transfer carrot to a blender or food processor and purée using reserved steaming water to achieve age-appropriate consistency.

4. In a small bowl, combine carrot purée with Sweet Potato Purée.

Apricot and Banana Mash

*Fresh apricots can be tart; sweet banana makes them easily
acceptable to baby's tastes.*

INGREDIENTS | YIELDS ¼ CUP

2 tablespoons Apricot Purée (see Chapter 3)
2 tablespoons Banana Mash (see Chapter 3)

In a small bowl, combine all ingredients.

Apricot and Apple Purée

Freezing leftover purées allows you to make combinations that take advantage of different growing seasons.

INGREDIENTS | YIELDS ¼ CUP

2 tablespoons Apricot Purée (see Chapter 3)
2 tablespoons Apple Purée (see Chapter 3)

In a small bowl, combine all ingredients.

Puréeing 101

When these recipes call for a purée, it means a solid food that has been turned into a smooth, almost liquid, consistency. Most soft fruits, plums, apricots, peaches, berries, and so on, can be washed, peeled (if they have a tougher skin, like peaches), and put in the food processor or blender. The juice in the fruit is probably adequate to achieve the right consistency without added water. Most vegetables will benefit from initial steaming before puréeing. Because vegetables are not as juicy as fruits, they might need some additional water or broth to achieve the right liquid texture.

Apple and Plum Compote

Use a sweet variety of apple for this dish, such as Golden Delicious, Fuji, or Pink Lady.

INGREDIENTS | YIELDS 2 CUPS

1 sweet apple
2 small plums
⅛ teaspoon ground cinnamon
Enough water to cover fruit

1. Peel apple and plums and cut into chunks.

2. In a large saucepan over medium heat, combine apple and plum chunks with cinnamon. Cover fruit with water. Cook until apples are very tender and start to break apart, approximately 10 minutes depending on the size of the chunks.

3. Mash with a potato masher or the back of a spoon. Transfer to blender or food processor if a finer consistency is needed.

Can You Still Go Out to Eat?

For you, more and more restaurants are featuring organic ingredients. For your baby, you can easily pack up his food and bring it out with you. Since babies aren't picky about their dinner being served at any exact temperature, so long as you keep it safe by packing the food along with an ice pack, you should be good to go.

Butternut Squash with Apples and Pears

Acorn squash or pumpkin can be substituted for butternut squash in this recipe.

INGREDIENTS | YIELDS 1 CUP

½ cup peeled butternut squash chunks
¼ cup water
2 tablespoons Apple Purée (see Chapter 3)
2 tablespoons Pear Purée (see Chapter 3)

1. In a medium saucepan, combine squash and water and bring to a boil. Stir while cooking to ensure that squash cooks evenly. Cook until tender, about 8–10 minutes.

2. Transfer squash to a food processor or blender. Purée, using reserved cooking water as necessary to achieve age-appropriate consistency.

3. In a medium bowl, combine squash with Apple Purée and Pear Purée.

Wash That Spoon!

To prevent contaminating a large batch of baby food, take out only what you think your baby will eat. Once the spoon has gone from your baby's mouth back into the bowl, leftovers must be discarded.

Butternut Squash with Carrots

This is a great recipe to make your baby in the fall when both of these foods are in season.

INGREDIENTS | YIELDS ¼ CUP

1 small butternut squash
2 tablespoons store-bought carrot purée

1. Steam squash, remove skin, and cut into 2" cubes.

2. In food processor or blender, add squash and process on and off until desired consistency reached.

3. Combine 2 tablespoons of resulting butternut squash purée with carrot purée and serve. Freeze remaining butternut squash in an ice-cube tray.

How Do You Cook a Squash?

Butternut squash can be steamed, microwaved, or baked. To steam a squash: Cut in half and place in steamer for 20–30 minutes. To microwave a squash: Put a peeled squash in the microwave with 3 tablespoons of water for 8 minutes. To bake a squash: Cut squash and place in shallow pan with water and bake for 20 minutes in the oven.

Mashed Turnip and Sweet Potato

Although the outside of turnips can be white,
purple, or green, the inside is all white.

INGREDIENTS | YIELDS ½ CUP

1 small turnip
2 tablespoons water
¼ cup Sweet Potato Purée (see Chapter 3)

1. Peel turnip and chop into small chunks.

2. In a small saucepan, combine turnip and water. Bring to a boil and cook until the turnip is tender, approximately 10 minutes depending on the size of the chunks.

3. Transfer turnip to a blender or food processor. Purée.

4. In a medium bowl, combine turnip purée with Sweet Potato Purée and serve.

Freezing Tips

Once you've frozen extra baby food in an ice cube tray, transfer the cubes to a freezer-safe bag or container. Be sure to put a label on the container describing the contents and adding the date. Fruits and vegetables can be frozen for up to six months, and meats can be frozen up to three months.

Peaches and Quinoa

Quinoa is a great addition to soups for your baby. Add a small amount of quinoa to your baby's favorite soup to give it a good texture.

INGREDIENTS | YIELDS 6 TABLESPOONS

¼ cup of Peach Purée (see Chapter 3)
1 tablespoon cooked Quinoa (see recipe in this chapter)

1. In a medium bowl, combine Peach Purée and cooked quinoa.

2. If necessary, use a food processor or blender until desired consistency reached.

Mother of All Grains

Quinoa has been grown in South America for more than 6,000 years. The Incas revered quinoa as the "mother of all grains" due to its unique nutritional properties. It has a good amount of balanced protein and is high in fiber, phosphorous, magnesium, and iron.

Avocado and Black Beans

In many Latin American countries, avocados and black beans are a first food!

INGREDIENTS | YIELDS ¼ CUP

2 tablespoons Black Bean Mash (see recipe in this chapter)
2 tablespoons Avocado Mash (see Chapter 3)

Combine ingredients in a small bowl and mash together with a fork.

Orzo and Sweet Pea Purée

Orzo *means "barley" in Italian. This rice-shaped pasta is not made of rice or barley, but from a hard-wheat semolina.*

INGREDIENTS | YIELDS 6 TABLESPOONS

¼ cup Sweet Pea Purée (see Chapter 3)
2 tablespoons cooked orzo pasta

1. In a medium bowl, combine Sweet Pea Purée and cooked orzo pasta.

2. If necessary, use a food processor or blender until desired consistency is reached.

Making a Risotto?

Orzo pasta can be a great substitute for Arborio rice in many different recipes. Due to the size and shape of orzo pasta, many people think that it is a rice. It is not but has a similar consistency and properties and works just as well in Arborio rice in risotto recipes. Liven up your risottos with a little orzo pasta!

Zucchini and Rice Cereal

Zucchini squash comes in many colors: yellow, light green, and dark green! Use different types of zucchini together for a colorful dish.

INGREDIENTS | YIELDS ¼ CUP

1 medium zucchini

2 tablespoons prepared iron-fortified oatmeal cereal (with either breast milk or formula)

1. Cut off ends of zucchini; do not peel.

2. Cut into slices and steam zucchini squash pieces for 4–6 minutes to soften.

3. Place zucchini in a food processor or blender, and process on and off until desired consistency is reached.

4. In a small bowl, combine 2 tablespoons of zucchini purée with 2 tablespoons of prepared iron-fortified cereal and serve. Freeze remaining zucchini purée in ice-cube trays.

Rice Cereal and Peach Purée

Peaches are the second largest commercial fruit crop in the United States. The first major commercial fruit product is apples.

INGREDIENTS | YIELDS 6 TABLESPOONS

3 tablespoons prepared iron-fortified oatmeal cereal (with either breast milk or formula)

3 tablespoons Peach Purée (see Chapter 3)

1. In a medium bowl, combine prepared rice cereal and Peach Purée.

2. If necessary, use a food processor or blender until desired consistency is reached.

Peachy Facts

Peaches are revered in China as a symbol of long life. Many people in the United States grow peaches in their yards. Peach trees produce a pink beautiful flower. Interestingly, the peach is the state flower of Delaware and the state fruit of South Carolina and Georgia. The state of Georgia calls itself the Peach State.

Apple and Banana Oatmeal Cereal

Most babies prefer the taste of sweet apples over tart, so it's best to stay away from Granny Smith apples when making apple purée for the earliest eaters.

INGREDIENTS | YIELDS 6 TABLESPOONS

2 tablespoons prepared iron-fortified oatmeal cereal (with either breast milk or formula)
2 tablespoons Apple Purée (see Chapter 3)
2 tablespoons Banana Mash (see Chapter 3)

In a medium bowl, combine all ingredients.

Pinto Beans and Brown Rice

You can use canned pinto beans or you can cook pinto beans from dry beans. If choosing canned beans, choose organic beans and make sure they do not contain hot peppers.

INGREDIENTS | YIELDS ¼ CUP

2 tablespoons cooked brown rice
2 tablespoons Refried Pinto Beans (see recipe in this chapter)

1. In a small bowl combine brown rice and pinto bean mash and mix well.

2. If necessary, use a food processor or blender until desired consistency reached.

Pinto Beans, Apples, and Barley

Apples add a little natural sweetness to this dish.

INGREDIENTS | YIELDS 6 TABLESPOONS

2 tablespoons prepared iron-fortified barley cereal (with either breast milk or formula)
2 tablespoons Refried Pinto Beans (see recipe in this chapter)
2 tablespoons Apple Purée (see Chapter 3)

In a medium bowl, combine all ingredients.

Island Breakfast Cereal

Using frozen fruit in winter when local options are limited can bring a taste of the tropics to an otherwise gloomy day.

INGREDIENTS | YIELDS 6 TABLESPOONS

2 tablespoons prepared iron-fortified barley cereal (with either breast milk or formula)
2 tablespoons Papaya Purée (see Chapter 3)
2 tablespoons Mango Purée (see Chapter 3)

In a medium bowl, combine all ingredients.

Thawing Frozen Purées

If you've frozen your purées in an ice cube tray, and then transferred them to a freezer-safe container, you have a collection of 2-tablespoon (1-ounce) servings of baby food. When it's time to thaw them, you can put the cubes you need in the refrigerator in the morning to thaw by evening, pack them with an ice pack in baby's diaper bag to be ready in a few hours, or microwave them, being sure to stir them well to eliminate hot spots. It's not safe to thaw the purée on the kitchen counter, as bacteria can start to grow in a partially defrosted cube.

Kasha with Peach and Pear Purée

*Once your child has tried each of these components individually,
have fun combining different combinations together to provide
variety to your child's developing taste buds.*

INGREDIENTS | YIELDS 6 TABLESPOONS

2 tablespoons Peach Purée (see Chapter 3)
2 tablespoons Pear Purée (see Chapter 3)
2 tablespoons cooked kasha cereal

1. In a medium bowl, combine all the ingredients.
2. If necessary, use a food processor or blender until desired consistency is reached.

Want to Stop Your Grains from Sticking Together?

Before cooking buckwheat, rice, millet, barley, or kasha, wash the grains first in warm water and then follow with hot water. Warm water removes the starch from the surface of grains. The hot water then removes the fat that may rise to the surface of grains during their storage.

Chicken with Cherries and Brown Rice

Cook a plain extra chicken breast when you cook dinner for your family to use in a purée for your infant.

INGREDIENTS | YIELDS 2 CUPS

6 cups water
1 small (4-ounce) boneless, skinless chicken breast
½ cup pitted cherries
1 cup cooked brown rice

1. In a large stockpot bring the 6 cups of water to a boil. Place chicken breast in pot and boil until done, approximately 10 minutes. Once done, remove from water, cut into small pieces, and allow to cool.

2. In a medium bowl, combine chicken pieces, cherries, and brown rice.

3. Use a food processor or blender until desired consistency is reached. Use broth from cooking the chicken, breast milk, or iron-fortified formula to reach an age-appropriate consistency. If consistency is too chunky, drain through a sieve and purée remaining liquid.

Chicken and Mango Purée

If fresh mangos are out of season, frozen mango can be substituted in this recipe.

INGREDIENTS | YIELDS 2 CUPS

6 cups water
1 small (4-ounce) boneless, skinless chicken breast
1 cup Mango Purée (see Chapter 3)

1. In a large stockpot bring 6 cups of water to a boil.

2. Place chicken breast in pot and boil until done, approximately 10 minutes.

3. Once done, remove from water, cut into small pieces, and allow to cool.

4. In a medium bowl, combine chicken and Mango Purée.

5. Use a food processor or blender until desired consistency is reached. Use broth from cooking the chicken, breast milk, or iron-fortified formula to reach an age-appropriate consistency.

6. If consistency is too chunky, drain through a sieve and purée remaining liquid.

Chicken, Banana, and Coconut Purée

This is a great dish for grownups, too! Cook the adult portion in a separate pot so that you can spice it up. Options to spice it up for adults include adding some red chili paste, diced onions, coconut milk, curry powder, and fresh cilantro. Serve over brown or Arborio rice.

INGREDIENTS | YIELDS 2 CUPS

6 cups water
1 small (4-ounce) boneless, skinless chicken breast
1 small banana or ½ large banana
1 teaspoon light coconut milk

1. In a large stockpot bring 6 cups of water to a boil. Place the chicken breast in the pot and boil until done, approximately 10 minutes.

2. Once done, remove from water, cut into small pieces, and allow to cool.

3. In a medium bowl, combine chicken, banana, and coconut milk.

4. Use a food processor or blender until desired consistency is reached. Use broth from cooking the chicken, breast milk, or iron-fortified formula to reach an age-appropriate consistency. If consistency is too chunky, drain through a sieve and purée remaining liquid.

Chicken, Papaya, and Nutmeg Mash

This recipe works best with a very ripe papaya. If your papaya is underripe then it will be necessary to cut it into cubes and steam it for about 5 minutes.

INGREDIENTS | YIELDS 2 CUPS

6 cups water
1 small (4-ounce) boneless, skinless chicken breast
½ cup cubed ripe papaya
2 tablespoons of breast milk or formula
Dash of ground nutmeg

1. In a stockpot, bring 6 cups of water to a boil. Place chicken breast in pot and boil until done, approximately 10 minutes.

2. Once done, remove from water, cut into small pieces, and allow to cool.

3. In a medium bowl, combine chicken, papaya, and nutmeg.

4. Use a food processor or blender until desired consistency is reached. Use broth from cooking the chicken, breast milk, or iron-fortified formula to reach an age-appropriate consistency. If consistency is too chunky, drain through a sieve and purée remaining liquid.

What Is the Best Way to Ripen a Papaya?
Place it in a brown paper bag with an apple for the fastest ripening. Apples produce ethylene gas, which speeds up ripening.

Chicken and Parsnip Purée

It is best to choose a small to medium-sized parsnip for this recipe. Large root vegetables have a tendency to be woody and bitter, which can turn some children off the taste of these vegetables.

INGREDIENTS | YIELDS 2 CUPS

1 medium-sized parsnip
1 cup water
1 small (4-ounce) cooked boneless, skinless chicken breast
3 tablespoons breast milk, iron-fortified formula, or water

1. Peel and dice parsnip. Bring 1 cup of water to a boil in a medium saucepan and cook parsnip until tender, about 15 minutes.

2. Cut cooked chicken into small pieces. In a medium bowl, combine chicken and parsnip.

3. Use a food processor or blender until desired consistency is reached. Use broth from cooking the chicken, breast milk, or iron-fortified formula to reach an age-appropriate consistency. If consistency is too chunky, drain through a sieve and purée remaining liquid.

Chicken, Carrot, and Sweet Onion Mash

Sweet onions are a nice way to introduce your child to the flavor and health benefits of onions.

INGREDIENTS | YIELDS 2 CUPS

6 cups water
1 small (4-ounce) boneless, skinless chicken breast
2 tablespoons chopped sweet onion
2 medium carrots, peeled
2 teaspoons olive oil

1. In a large pot, bring 6 cups of water to a boil.

2. Preheat oven to 400°F.

3. Add chicken and onion to water and boil until done, approximately 10 minutes. Once done, drain chicken and onions and save. Cut chicken into small pieces and allow to cool.

4. Cut carrots lengthwise and then into small pieces, coat the pieces with olive oil and place on a baking sheet. Roast in oven for 15–20 minutes.

5. In a medium bowl, combine chicken, onions, and roasted carrots.

6. Use a food processor or blender until desired consistency is reached. Use broth from cooking the chicken to reach an age-appropriate consistency. If consistency is too chunky, drain through a sieve and purée remaining liquid.

Beef Stew Mash

Most of your family stew recipes can be transformed into baby foods. Just limit the amount of spices and make sure the ingredients are age appropriate. You can purée just about any food for your child!

INGREDIENTS | YIELDS 1 CUP

2 ounces stew beef

2 cups water

1 medium carrot, scrubbed and sliced

½ medium-sized russet potato, peeled and diced

1. In a medium-sized heavy saucepan, brown the beef on all sides.

2. In a small saucepan, bring 2 cups of water to a simmering boil. Add beef, cover, and cook for 20 minutes.

3. Add carrot and potato and cook another 15 minutes or until all ingredients are falling apart. Remove from heat and cool slightly.

4. Use a food processor or blender until desired consistency is reached. Use broth from cooking the beef to reach age-appropriate consistency. If consistency is too chunky, drain through a sieve and purée remaining liquid.

Beef and Barley

For a shortcut, you could buy precooked beef from the store.

INGREDIENTS | YIELDS ½ CUP

2 ounces of stew beef or other cut, cooked beef
3 tablespoons cooked pearl barley
2 tablespoons store-bought carrot purée

1. Cut beef into small pieces. In a medium bowl, combine cooked beef, barley, and carrot purée together.

2. Use a food processor or blender until desired consistency is reached. Use beef or vegetable broth to reach an age-appropriate consistency. If consistency is too chunky, drain through a fine-mesh sieve and purée.

Baby Food in a Slow Cooker?

Slow cookers are a great way to make baby foods. Place your meats, vegetables, spices, and water in a slow cooker. Turn it on and forget about it until later in the day. Meats and vegetables get cooked to a wonderful texture for puréeing. When done, purée the stew, serve, and then freeze the leftovers.

Minced Pork Chop with Applesauce

Make this as a family dinner for your whole family. Once the pork is cooked, purée the pork with apple purée for your infant. This allows you to not make extra meals for your infant but use what you are preparing for the rest of the family.

INGREDIENTS | YIELDS 2 CUPS

1 (8-ounce) cooked pork chop
1 cup Apple Purée (see Chapter 3)

1. Cut pork chop into small pieces.

2. In a medium bowl, combine pork and Apple Purée together.

3. Use a food processor or blender until desired consistency is reached. Use chicken or vegetable broth to reach an age-appropriate consistency. If consistency is too chunky, drain through a sieve and purée remaining liquid.

Is There Iron in Pork?

Yes! There is 0.9 mg of iron in 1 ounce of pork. This iron is heme iron, which is better absorbed by the body than plant sources of iron. Try to feed your baby two sources of iron-containing foods per day. For example, iron-fortified rice cereal in the morning and a meal containing meat later in the day.

Poached Fish and Carrots

Be sure to choose low-mercury and environmentally friendly fish for this recipe.

INGREDIENTS | YIELDS 2 CUPS

¼ pound tilapia (U.S.-farmed)
1 cup store-bought puréed carrots

1. Fill sauté pan with about 1"–2" water and bring to a boil. Add fish, cover, turn heat down to low, and allow to poach for 5–10 minutes.

2. Once done, drain fish, saving small amount of liquid, and chop. Ensure no bones remain in fish.

3. In a medium bowl, combine fish and carrot purée. Use a food processor or blender until desired consistency is reached. Use broth from cooking the fish to reach an age-appropriate consistency. If consistency is too chunky, drain through a sieve and purée remaining liquid.

> **Healthy Fish**
>
> The Shedd Aquarium in Chicago produces a "Right Bite" guide, which shows you which fish are abundant, well cared for, and caught or farmed in environmentally friendly ways.

Lamb and Pumpkin Mash

Lamb is a good source of zinc. Zinc is important for a high-functioning immune system and it is vital for your child's growth. Your child's body needs zinc to grow as tall as she genetically can!

INGREDIENTS | YIELDS 2 CUPS

1 teaspoon olive oil
2 ounces ground lamb
½ cup canned pumpkin

1. In a medium saucepan with a teaspoon of olive oil, brown lamb meat until done. Browning the lamb should take about 5 minutes for this small amount.

2. Remove lamb from pan and combine with the pumpkin.

3. Use a food processor or blender until desired consistency is reached. Use vegetable or chicken broth to obtain an age-appropriate consistency.

4. If consistency is too chunky, drain through a fine-mesh sieve.

CHAPTER 5

Nine to Twelve Months

Lentil Soup

Divide this soup and freeze in small portions to have meals ready for the future.

INGREDIENTS | YIELDS 6 CUPS

1 tablespoon olive oil
1 clove garlic
¾ cup diced sweet onion
4 cups water
1 bouillon cube (vegetable, chicken, or beef)
1 cup diced carrots
½ cup diced celery
½ cup lentils
2 cups diced tomatoes with liquid

1. In a large stockpot, heat olive oil over medium-high heat.
2. Add garlic and onion and sauté for 5 minutes.
3. Add water, bouillon cube, carrots, and celery.
4. Rinse and pick over lentils, and add to pot.
5. Add tomatoes to pot.
6. Cover and simmer for 45 minutes.

A Soup a Day

Soups are fantastic bases for infant meals. It is easy to incorporate many different vegetables in soups that your child may not adventure to taste on his own. The consistency of soup is ideal for making purées once soup is done, or puréeing to different thicker consistencies as your child grows and develops.

Split Pea Soup

This protein-rich soup is also a good source of vitamin A, vitamin C, potassium, and dietary fiber.

INGREDIENTS | YIELDS 6 CUPS

1 cup dried green split peas
1 medium sweet onion
1 medium carrot, peeled
1 medium baking potato, peeled
1 teaspoon olive oil
3 cups vegetable broth
¼ teaspoon dried summer savory
⅛ teaspoon ground cumin
1 bay leaf

1. Pick over split peas and remove any debris. Rinse, drain, and set aside.

2. Finely chop onion, carrot, and potato.

3. In a stockpot, heat olive oil over medium-high heat. Add vegetables and sauté until soft, approximately 3 minutes. Add remaining ingredients. Stir. Simmer uncovered for 40 minutes, or until split peas are very soft. Remove bay leaf. Add more vegetable broth for a thinner soup, if desired.

Different Tastes and Textures

The first year of eating is about getting used to new tastes and textures. Set the groundwork for good eating habits by exposing your baby to a variety of flavors, textures, and combinations. Throw away notions of what foods go together and be creative.

Vegetable Rice Soup

This soup cooks up thick, so it's easy to keep on the spoon for feeding. It also works well for an older baby who is learning self-feeding skills.

INGREDIENTS | YIELDS 10 CUPS

1 medium carrot, peeled
1 stalk celery
1 small russet potato, peeled
½ small sweet onion
1 small sweet potato, peeled
1 cup chopped spinach
1 cup brown rice
8 cups water
1 (15-ounce) can diced tomatoes
½ teaspoon dried oregano
½ teaspoon dried basil
½ teaspoon dried thyme

1. Finely chop all vegetables.

2. Combine all ingredients in a large stock pot. Bring to a boil. Reduce heat, cover, and simmer for 45 minutes or until rice is soft.

Flexible Grains

There is very little as frustrating as starting a recipe, confident that you have all of the ingredients on hand, and then discovering that you're missing a key component of your dish. Not to worry, because there is often a fine substitute right at hand. If you don't have brown rice, substitute white rice, orzo, barley, or quinoa.

Tomato and Orzo Soup

This is an easy way to turn a can of soup into a family meal.

INGREDIENTS | YIELDS 6 CUPS

4 cups roasted red pepper and tomato soup

1 cup canned black beans, drained

2 cups cooked orzo pasta

6 tablespoons whole-milk plain yogurt

1. Combine soup and beans in a medium saucepan over medium heat. Mix to combine.

2. Add pasta to saucepan and stir. Cook until warmed through.

3. Top each serving with 1 tablespoon yogurt.

Will Your Baby Get Fat From Eating Fat?

No! Babies need adequate fat in their diets to grow properly and foster brain development. Do not be shy about adding fat to your baby's meals. In fact, infant food labels do not list calories from fat, saturated fat, or cholesterol content in order to prevent parents from limiting foods high in fat that babies need.

Split Pea Curry

This dish is inspired by the flavorful curries that make up the heart of Indian cooking.

INGREDIENTS | YIELDS 5 CUPS

1 cup dried green split peas
1 cup cauliflower florets
2 small baking potatoes
½ cup peeled and diced carrots
1 clove garlic, minced
2 cups water or vegetable broth
½ cup tomato sauce
1½ teaspoons curry powder

1. Pick over split peas and remove any debris. Rinse, drain, and set aside. Dice cauliflower and potatoes.

2. Combine all ingredients in a large sauté pan or stockpot. Simmer for 45–60 minutes, or until tender.

Making the Most of a Slow Cooker

Even parents with the best of intentions for providing home-cooked organic meals for their families can become overwhelmed by all of the demands that life with a baby brings. A slow cooker can be a great tool to help reduce some of that pressure. Soups, casseroles, and curries can be assembled during a nap or the night before and then cooked unattended for 6–8 hours.

Alphabet Noodle Soup

As your children get older, use alphabet soup to help them learn the alphabet. Who ever said that eating can't be educational?

INGREDIENTS | YIELDS 8 CUPS

10 cups water
1 large broiler-fryer chicken
3–4 stalks celery, chopped
4–6 medium carrots, peeled and chopped
1 large sweet onion, chopped
1–2 medium tomatoes, chopped
¼ teaspoon salt, or to taste
¼ teaspoon black pepper, or to taste
2 bay leaves
2 teaspoons chicken bouillon
1½ cups cooked alphabet noodles

1. Bring water to a boil. Add chicken and return to a boil. Add more water if necessary to cover chicken.

2. Once boiling, reduce heat immediately. Skim off any fat from the top of soup.

3. Add remaining ingredients and simmer for 1½ hours.

4. Remove chicken and save for another use. Remove all vegetables and discard bay leaves.

5. Strain soup and allow to cool. Once cool, skim off hardened fat.

6. Reheat soup and add cooked alphabet noodles. Serve.

Chicken Noodle Soup

Chicken noodle soup is a great method to introduce chicken to your child. Cut pieces of chicken very tiny to avoid choking. Boiling the chicken in this soup gets the meat perfectly tender for your baby.

INGREDIENTS | YIELDS 8 CUPS

1 pound boneless, skinless chicken breasts cut into ¼" pieces

½ red onion, diced

2 stalks celery, sliced

1 medium carrot, peeled and sliced

¼ red bell pepper, diced

3 cloves garlic, minced

2 tablespoons butter or trans fat–free margarine

2 tablespoons olive or canola oil

¼ cup all-purpose flour

1 teaspoon dried basil

½ teaspoon dried oregano

⅛ teaspoon black pepper

3 (14.5-ounce) cans chicken broth

1 (14.5-ounce) can diced tomatoes, undrained

½ summer squash or zucchini, sliced

6 ounces uncooked whole-wheat spiral pasta

5 ounces fresh spinach, chopped

1. In a large saucepan over medium heat, sauté chicken, onion, celery, carrot, red pepper, and garlic in butter and oil for 5 minutes.

2. Stir in flour, basil, oregano, and pepper until blended.

3. Slowly add chicken broth, tomatoes, and zucchini.

4. Bring to a boil. Reduce heat; cover and simmer for 1 hour.

5. Return to a boil; stir in the pasta and spinach.

6. Reduce heat; simmer, uncovered, for 12–15 minutes or until pasta is tender.

Blueberry Mini Muffins

Fresh or frozen blueberries work well in this recipe. If you are using frozen, the batter will take on a purple hue unless you thaw them first.

INGREDIENTS | YIELDS 42 MINI MUFFINS

2 cups white whole-wheat flour
1½ teaspoons baking powder, divided
½ teaspoon salt
½ cup applesauce
½ cup flaxseed meal
¼ cup canola oil
½ teaspoon vanilla extract
¾ cup apple juice concentrate
¼ cup plain yogurt (dairy or soy)
¼ cup whole milk (dairy or soy)
1½ cups blueberries

1. Preheat oven to 350°F. Lightly oil mini muffin pans.
2. In a medium bowl, combine flour, 1 teaspoon baking powder, and salt.
3. In a large bowl, combine applesauce with ½ teaspoon baking powder.
4. Add flaxseed meal, oil, vanilla, apple juice concentrate, yogurt, and milk to applesauce. Combine well.
5. Slowly add dry ingredients to wet and stir to combine. Fold in blueberries.
6. Spoon batter into prepared mini muffin pans.
7. Bake for 25–30 minutes, or until a toothpick inserted into the center of a muffin comes out clean.

Banana Bread

This banana bread has a great texture and a not-too-sweet banana flavor.

INGREDIENTS | YIELDS 1 LOAF

2 cups white whole-wheat flour
1 tablespoon plus ½ teaspoon baking powder, divided
1 teaspoon baking soda
¾ teaspoon salt
½ cup applesauce
½ cup butter or trans fat–free margarine, softened
2 tablespoons apple juice concentrate
⅓ cup agave nectar
1 teaspoon vanilla extract
4 ripe medium bananas

1. Preheat oven to 350°F. Lightly oil a standard loaf pan.

2. In a medium bowl combine flour, 1 tablespoon baking powder, baking soda, and salt.

3. In a large bowl, combine applesauce with ½ teaspoon baking powder.

4. Add butter or margarine, apple juice concentrate, agave nectar, and vanilla to applesauce and mix well.

5. In a medium bowl mash bananas. Mix bananas into wet ingredients.

6. Slowly mix dry ingredients into wet.

7. Pour batter into prepared loaf pan.

8. Bake 1 hour or until a toothpick inserted into the center of the loaf comes out clean.

9. Cool 10 minutes in pan, then cool completely on cooling rack.

Apple and Sweet Potato Mini Muffins

Because these muffins aren't too sweet they're great as a take-along snack, warmed and topped with butter or Sweet Potato Spread (see recipe in this chapter).

INGREDIENTS | YIELDS 42 MINI MUFFINS

2 cups white whole-wheat flour
1½ teaspoons baking powder, divided
½ teaspoon salt
½ teaspoon ground cinnamon
½ cup applesauce
½ cup flaxseed meal
¼ cup canola oil
½ teaspoon vanilla extract
½ cup whole milk (dairy or soy)
1 cup frozen apple juice concentrate
1½ cups grated sweet potato
1 cup grated apple

1. Preheat oven to 350°F. Lightly oil mini muffin pans.
2. In a medium bowl, combine flour, 1 teaspoon baking powder, salt, and cinnamon.
3. In a large bowl, combine applesauce with ½ teaspoon baking powder.
4. Add flaxseed meal, oil, vanilla, milk, and apple juice concentrate to applesauce. Stir to combine.
5. Slowly mix dry ingredients into wet until combined.
6. Mix in sweet potato and apple.
7. Pour batter into prepared mini muffin pans.
8. Bake for 25–30 minutes or until a toothpick inserted in the middle of a muffin comes out dry.

Carrot and Zucchini Mini Muffins

What a fun way for baby to eat vegetables!
Mini muffins are just the right size for little fingers.

INGREDIENTS | YIELDS 42 MINI MUFFINS

2 cups white whole-wheat flour
1½ teaspoons baking powder, divided
½ teaspoon salt
1 teaspoon ground cinnamon
½ cup applesauce
½ cup flaxseed meal
¼ cup canola oil
½ teaspoon vanilla extract
¼ packed cup light brown sugar
½ cup maple syrup
1 cup peeled and grated carrots
1 cup grated zucchini

1. Preheat oven to 350°F. Lightly oil mini muffin pans.
2. In a medium mixing bowl, combine flour, 1 teaspoon baking powder, salt, and cinnamon.
3. In a large bowl, combine applesauce with ½ teaspoon baking powder. Add flaxseed meal, oil, vanilla, brown sugar, and syrup.
4. Slowly mix dry ingredients into wet. Mix in carrots and zucchini.
5. Spoon batter into prepared mini muffin pans.
6. Bake for 15–20 minutes or until a toothpick inserted into the center of a muffin comes out clean.

Oatmeal with Cinnamon Apples

This hearty dish is great in the fall when apples are abundant. Pick apples at your local apple farm and use them for breakfast!

INGREDIENTS | YIELDS 2 CUPS

½ cup water

½ cup apple juice

1 Golden Delicious apple, peeled, cored, and chopped

⅔ cup rolled oats

1 teaspoon ground cinnamon

1–2 tablespoons light agave nectar

1 cup whole milk (dairy or soy)

1. In a small saucepan, combine water, apple juice, and apple. Bring to a boil.

2. Once boiling, stir in rolled oats and cinnamon. Return to a boil.

3. Reduce heat to low and simmer to desired thickness, about 3–5 minutes.

4. Add agave nectar to reach desired sweetness.

5. Pour milk over servings, and serve.

Limiting Salt and Sugar

Habits, whether good or bad, can begin early. Since babies don't have preconceived notions about how specific foods are "supposed" to taste, let them taste the purity of the high-quality organic ingredients you are using. Babies don't expect foods to be salty or sweet, so if they aren't introduced to excessive salt and sugar, they can develop the good habit of liking food the way nature intended it to taste.

Yogurt Berry Parfait

Wheat germ contains a small amount of fat, which makes it spoil quickly. Store your wheat germ in the fridge to extend its life.

INGREDIENTS | YIELDS 2 CUPS

1¼ teaspoons wheat germ

1 cup vanilla yogurt

1 cup seasonal berries

1. Pour wheat germ into the yogurt and mix well.

2. In a glass, alternate layers of yogurt and berries.

Is Wheat Germ a Germ?

Wheat germ is the "embryo" part of the wheat kernel. Wheat germ will become the sprout to grow into wheat grass. It is a very nutritious part of the wheat kernel and contains the following nutrients: vitamin E, folic acid, magnesium, phosphorus, thiamine, zinc. It also contains essential fatty acids and is a good source of fiber.

Strawberry Banana Yogurt

This recipe makes a great side dish to go with Moist Yogurt Pancakes, which can be found in Chapter 6.

INGREDIENTS | YIELDS 2 CUPS

1 cup vanilla yogurt
½ cup strawberries
½ medium banana
½ teaspoon ground cinnamon

In a medium bowl, combine all ingredients.

Blueberry Syrup

Serve this delicious syrup over whole-grain waffles.
Your toddler will love it!

INGREDIENTS | YIELDS 2 CUPS

2 cups blueberries
⅓ cup apple juice concentrate
1 tablespoon cornstarch
2 tablespoons cold water

1. In a small saucepan over medium heat, combine blueberries and apple juice concentrate. Simmer for 10 minutes.

2. While the fruit is simmering, combine cornstarch and water in a small bowl.

3. Add cornstarch and water mixture to blueberries.

4. Simmer and stir continuously, until thickened.

Blueberries on Ice

Freezing blueberries at home is a great way to make the taste of summer last all year. Wash the blueberries, dry them, and pick out any damaged berries. Then, spread out the berries on a baking sheet and freeze. Once frozen solid, transfer the berries to a freezer-safe container, where they can be enjoyed for up to six months.

Oatmeal with Sautéed Plantains

Plantains are a Central American staple; they can be cooked in sweet or savory dishes.

INGREDIENTS | YIELDS 2 CUP

1 medium yellow plantain (very ripe)
1 tablespoon brown sugar
1 teaspoon butter
½ cup water
½ cup apple juice
⅔ cup rolled oats
1 teaspoon ground cinnamon

1. Peel and cut plantain into ½" pieces.
2. Put brown sugar in a zip-top plastic bag and place plantain pieces in bag, shaking the bag to coat them.
3. Heat butter in small skillet over medium heat, place plantains in pan and cook until the sugar begins to caramelize, about 2 minutes each side; remove from heat.
4. In a small saucepan, combine water and apple juice. Bring to a boil.
5. Once boiling, stir in rolled oats and cinnamon. Return to a boil.
6. Reduce heat to low and simmer to desired thickness, about 3–5 minutes.
7. Top oat mixture with sautéed plantains and serve.

Plantains versus Bananas

Plantains are firmer and have a lower sugar content than bananas. Plantains need to be cooked but bananas are mostly eaten raw. In tropical areas of the world, plantains are often a first food for babies. Plantains are a staple item in these areas and are consumed on a daily basis.

Mashed Potatoes and Parsnips

Yukon gold potatoes have a rich flavor,
creamy texture, and beautiful color.

INGREDIENTS | YIELDS 3 CUPS

4 medium Yukon gold potatoes, peeled
2 medium parsnips, peeled
Water to cover
1 tablespoon olive oil
¼ teaspoon salt, optional

1. Roughly chop vegetables and place in a medium saucepan. Cover with water.

2. Bring mixture to a boil then reduce heat to a simmer. Cook until vegetables are tender, approximately 10–15 minutes depending on size of chopped pieces.

3. Drain, reserving cooking liquid.

4. Return vegetables to pot, mash with a potato masher or fork, and stir in olive oil, and salt if using.

5. Add reserved cooking water, 1 tablespoon at a time, until mash is the desired consistency.

Parsnips, a Late-Fall Treat

Parsnips look very similar to white carrots. Because they are at their sweetest after having been exposed to cold temperatures, they are best in the late fall or early winter. Cook them in the same way as carrots for great-tasting results.

Black Bean and Carrot Mash

The addition of carrots to the black beans is a great way to boost the vitamin A content of the black beans.

INGREDIENTS | YIELDS 2½ CUPS

1 (5-ounce) can black beans, rinsed and drained
½ cup store-bought puréed carrots

1. In a medium saucepan, combine black beans and carrot purée over medium heat.
2. Allow black beans to soften, about 5–10 minutes.
3. Mash mixture with a potato masher while cooking on stove.
4. Remove from heat and serve.

Black Beans As a Superfood?

Black beans contain the same amount of antioxidants as grapes and cranberries. The darker the beans, the more antioxidants they contain. Also, looking for an iron-rich food for your baby? Look no further than black beans. They contain almost 4 grams of iron per cup of black beans.

Mango and Brown Rice

For a twist to this recipe, cook the brown rice in coconut milk to give this dish more of an Asian influence and introduce your child to the flavor of coconut!

INGREDIENTS | YIELDS 5 CUPS

2 cups cooked brown rice
2 medium mangos, chopped
1 tablespoon lime juice

1. In a medium bowl, combine cooked brown rice and chopped mangos.

2. Drizzle lime juice on top for flavor.

Healthiest Oil on Earth?

Coconut oil has a high amount of medium-chain triglycerides (MCT). These oils are hard to find in our diet. MCT oil is processed differently from the long-chain fats that are in animal products. These MCT oils may have a positive effect on cholesterol and heart disease. Small amounts of coconut oil can be part of a healthy diet.

Tofu Bites

Who needs highly processed chicken nuggets, when these tasty, high-protein treats are so easy to make?

INGREDIENTS | YIELDS 24 BITES

2 teaspoons olive oil
1 pound tofu (firm or extra-firm)
¼ cup whole-wheat flour
1 teaspoon garlic pepper

1. Preheat oven to 425°F. Grease a baking sheet with oil.
2. Drain tofu and cut into 24 rectangle-shaped bites.
3. Combine flour and garlic pepper in a shallow bowl. Dredge each tofu bite in the flour mixture.
4. Place coated triangles on prepared baking sheet.
5. Bake for 10 minutes or until golden brown.

Cauliflower and Potato Mash

Here is a twist on mashed potatoes! Add other items to these "mashed potatoes" based on your child's taste. Try adding peas to this mash for a little more texture.

INGREDIENTS | YIELDS 5 CUPS

2 large russet potatoes, peeled and chopped
1 medium head cauliflower, cut into florets
1 cup whole milk (dairy or soy)
1 tablespoon butter or trans fat–free margarine

1. Place potatoes in a medium-sized pot and cover with water. Boil the potatoes for 10 minutes until soft; drain, and return to pot.

2. Steam the cauliflower until tender; drain, and add to pot with potatoes.

3. Add milk and butter to potatoes and cauliflower.

4. Mash with a potato masher or use a beater to get a thinner purée.

The Different Colors of Cauliflower

There are many colors of cauliflower. Purple cauliflower contains the anti-oxidant anthocyanin, which is also in red wine and cabbage. Green cauli-flower is called broccoflower. And orange cauliflower contains twenty-five times the amount of vitamin A that is in white cauliflower . . . it competes well with carrots.

Roast Lamb, Rice, and Tomato Compote

This recipe helps you use the lamb that you're serving the whole family in an appropriate way for your baby.

INGREDIENTS | YIELDS 1 CUP

2 ounces roasted lamb meat
¼ cup cooked brown rice
¼ cup Sweet Potato Purée (see Chapter 3)
¼ cup diced tomatoes

Purée all ingredients in a blender or food processor.

Avoiding Hot Spots

Some babies prefer their food to be slightly warmed. The microwave can be a convenient tool for heating up your baby's food. Be careful, though, to stir the food thoroughly, because the microwave can cause some spots in the food to be much hotter than other spots. Test the food it once it's stirred to be sure that it's not too hot for baby's sensitive mouth.

Coconut Pineapple Rice Pudding

With these three ingredients in the pantry, making this tasty, wholesome dessert is a snap.

INGREDIENTS | YIELDS 4 CUPS

1 cup Arborio rice
1 (15-ounce) can light coconut milk
1 (15-ounce) can crushed pineapple in juice

1. Preheat oven to 325°F.

2. Rinse rice and place in casserole dish.

3. In a small saucepan, bring coconut milk and crushed pineapple with juice to a boil. Add to rice in casserole dish and stir to combine.

4. Cover and bake for 1 hour.

Barbecue Tofu and Quinoa

Quinoa and tofu combine for a protein-rich meal with a lot of flavor.

INGREDIENTS | YIELDS 5 CUPS

1 pound firm or extra-firm tofu
1 cup mushroom caps (button or cremini)
¼ small sweet onion
1 large red bell pepper
1 tablespoon olive oil
½ cup barbecue sauce
2 cups cooked quinoa

1. Cut tofu into 1" cubes.

2. Dice mushrooms, onion, and red pepper.

3. Heat olive oil over high heat in a medium skillet, then add tofu. Cook 3 minutes, turning tofu as it cooks. Add diced vegetables and cook 5 minutes more.

4. Add barbecue sauce and cook 5 more minutes. Serve over prepared quinoa.

Simple Barbecue Sauce

To make a tasty, basic barbecue sauce, combine ¼ cup soy sauce, 2 tablespoons blackstrap molasses, 3 tablespoons honey or agave nectar, and ¼ cup ketchup.

Roasted Potato Rounds

*Baking potatoes or Yukon gold potatoes can
be substituted for red potatoes.*

INGREDIENTS | YIELDS 24 ROUNDS

3 large red potatoes
2 tablespoons olive oil, divided
Sprinkling of sea salt

1. Preheat oven to 475°F.

2. Wash and thinly slice potatoes.

3. Spread 1 tablespoon olive oil on baking sheet. Spread potato slices on top of oil. Top with remaining oil and salt.

4. Bake for 13–15 minutes, until soft and golden.

Mashed Sweet Potatoes

*If part of your sweet potato is bad, you cannot just
remove the bad part and use the rest of the potato.
If part of it is bad, you have to get rid of the whole potato!*

INGREDIENTS | YIELDS 4 CUPS

4 medium sweet potatoes
2 tablespoons butter or trans fat–free margarine

1. Cube and peel sweet potatoes.

2. Bring a pot of water to a boil. Place potatoes in boiling water and boil for about 20 minutes. Drain potatoes and place in mixing bowl.

3. Add butter to potatoes and mash.

Organic Farmer's Pie

Serve this tender casserole with Easy Gravy (see recipe in this chapter) and Homemade Applesauce (see Chapter 4) for an autumnal feast.

INGREDIENTS | YIELDS A 3-QUART CASSEROLE DISH

2 large sweet potatoes, peeled and diced
Water to cover
1 tablespoon olive oil
2 cloves garlic, minced
¼ cup grated sweet onion
¼ cup grated zucchini
¼ cup grated carrot
3 cups veggie burger crumbles
½ cup plain yogurt (dairy or soy)
½ teaspoon salt

1. Preheat oven to 350°F.

2. In a large saucepan, cover sweet potatoes with water. Bring to a boil; boil uncovered until tender, approximately 20 minutes.

3. While potatoes are cooking, heat olive oil on medium in a medium skillet.

4. Add garlic and vegetables. Sauté until soft, approximately 5 minutes.

5. Add veggie burger crumbles and heat through.

6. When sweet potatoes are tender, drain and return them to the pot. Mash the sweet potatoes with yogurt and salt using a potato masher or fork.

7. Scrape the burger mixture into a 3-quart casserole dish.

8. Spread the sweet potatoes on top.

9. Bake uncovered for 40 minutes.

Easy Gravy

For many young eaters, sauces and dips make every dish more exciting. This easy gravy can dress up many different entrées, from Organic Farmer's Pie (see recipe in this chapter) to broiled chicken.

INGREDIENTS | YIELDS 1 CUP

1 bouillon cube (vegetable, chicken, or beef)
1 cup plus 2 tablespoons water
2 teaspoons low-sodium soy sauce
¼ teaspoon poultry seasoning
1 tablespoon cornstarch

1. Dissolve bouillon cube in 1 cup boiling water in a small bowl.
2. Add soy sauce and poultry seasoning to bouillon.
3. In a separate small bowl, thoroughly combine cornstarch with 2 tablespoons water.
4. Add diluted cornstarch to bouillon mixture, stirring until combined and thickened.

Sauces Can Make Dinnertime Easier

Around 18 months, even the easiest eater can start to be picky. Diets that used to be rich with fruits, vegetables, grains, and proteins can whittle down to just a few items in what seems like the blink of an eye. Offering a favorite sauce, whether it's ketchup, gravy, or dip can keep little ones eating a greater variety. While ketchup-dipped cantaloupe probably sounds unappealing to an adult, it might just be a culinary delight to a child.

Vegetable Barley Casserole

For a variation, stir in one cup shredded, boiled chicken after the casserole is finished.

INGREDIENTS | YIELDS 4½ CUPS

3 medium carrots
1 bunch kale
3¼ cups water, divided
1 bouillon cube (vegetable, chicken, or beef)
1 cup pearl barley
½ small sweet onion, diced

1. Preheat oven to 350°F.
2. Peel and thinly slice carrots. Thoroughly wash and dry kale. Trim and remove stems.
3. In a food processor, finely chop kale.
4. Add ¼ cup water to chopped kale 2 tablespoons at a time to make a paste.
5. In a small saucepan, bring 3 cups water to a boil.
6. Dissolve bouillon cube in boiling water.
7. Combine all ingredients in a 3-quart casserole dish.
8. Cover and bake for 1½ hours.

Lentils with Spinach and Quinoa

You do not want to mix old lentils with new lentils. The older lentils are, the longer they take to cook. Lentils will cook unevenly if you mix old and new lentils.

INGREDIENTS | YIELDS 2 CUPS

1 cup dried lentils
½ cup quinoa
1 cup water
½ teaspoon garlic
1 teaspoon olive oil
4 cups vegetable broth, to cover lentils
3 cups fresh spinach

1. Pick over lentils and remove any debris. Set aside.

2. Add quinoa and water to a microwaveable glass bowl. Cover and heat on high for 4 minutes. Remove from microwave and stir. Heat again for 2 minutes, stir, and let stand for 1 minute.

3. In a medium pan over low heat, sauté garlic and oil until translucent, about 3–5 minutes.

4. Add lentils to pan, cover with vegetable broth, increase heat to medium-high and bring to a boil for 2–3 minutes. Reduce heat to medium and cook until the lentils are tender.

5. When lentils are tender, add spinach to broth. Allow spinach to soften to desired consistency.

6. Drain lentils and spinach. Combine quinoa with the lentil and spinach mixture. Serve.

> ## Lentil Cooking Tips
> Do not add salt to the water when cooking your lentils as it might toughen the beans. Also, wait to add any acidic items to lentils until late in the cooking process as acidic foods make lentils take longer to cook.

Whole-Wheat Shells
with Marinara Sauce

*You can also use this sauce in the
Italian Eggplant recipe (see Chapter 6).*

INGREDIENTS | YIELDS 3 CUPS OF SAUCE

1 tablespoon olive oil
1 clove garlic, minced
2½ cups diced tomatoes (or 1 [28-ounce] can diced tomatoes, drained)
6 tablespoons tomato paste
1 teaspoon agave nectar
1 tablespoon chopped fresh basil (or 1 teaspoon dried basil)
1 teaspoon dried oregano
Cooked whole-wheat shells

1. In a medium saucepan, heat olive oil over medium heat. Add garlic and sauté for 2 minutes until fragrant.

2. Add tomatoes, paste, agave nectar, basil, and oregano; stir thoroughly.

3. Simmer uncovered for approximately 1 hour or until desired texture.

4. Serve sauce over whole-wheat pasta.

Broccoli and Quinoa Casserole

This dish is genuine comfort food that has a great consistency for a younger child, but will please the rest of the family as well. By combining the cooked ingredients without an added baking step, the dish remains very tender and easy for little ones to manage.

INGREDIENTS | YIELDS 6 CUPS

1 cup creamy corn soup
½ cup shredded Cheddar cheese (dairy or soy)
1 large bunch of broccoli
3 cups cooked quinoa

1. In a small saucepan, heat soup over medium-high heat. Add cheese and stir until melted. Set aside.

2. Cut broccoli into small florets and steam until tender. Combine quinoa, cheese sauce, and broccoli in a serving bowl or casserole dish.

Is Quinoa a Grain?

Although quinoa looks like a grain and cooks like a grain, it is not a true cereal grain. It is actually the seeds of the chenopodium or goosefoot plant. Its relatives include beets, spinach, and Swiss chard.

Chickpea, Carrot, and Cauliflower Mash

Cauliflower contains many cancer-fighting nutrients, so start your baby off on the right foot with this tasty recipe.

INGREDIENTS | YIELDS 4 CUPS

2 medium carrots, peeled and sliced
1 cup cauliflower florets
2 cups cooked chickpeas (or 1 [15-ounce] can)
¼ cup vegetable broth or water

1. Steam carrots and cauliflower until very tender.
2. Drain and rinse chickpeas.
3. In a medium bowl, combine all ingredients and mash with a potato masher or fork.
4. Add broth or water as necessary to reach an age-appropriate consistency.

Chicken, Sweet Pea, and Sweet Potato Dinner

If you're making a soup with chicken, take some of the chicken meat out, purée it, and freeze it for dishes like this. You'll still have plenty of chicken in the original soup, and you'll buy yourself a quick and easy dinner option down the line.

INGREDIENTS | YIELDS ¾ CUP

2 ounces boiled, shredded chicken
¼ cup Sweet Pea Purée (see Chapter 3)
¼ cup Sweet Potato Purée (see Chapter 3)

1. Purée chicken in a food processor or blender. Add water or broth as needed to achieve a smooth purée.
2. Combine chicken purée with vegetable purées in a medium bowl.

Cool Meats, Dude

Having a hard time blending your meats into purées? Meats tend to blend better if you wait until they cool to purée them. This is especially true with meats that have been baked instead of boiled. Boiled meats shred nicely, which can make puréeing them a little easier.

Hummus

This creamy, mild hummus is just right for younger taste buds.

INGREDIENTS | YIELDS 2 CUPS

2 cups cooked garbanzo beans (homemade or canned)
2 teaspoons lemon juice
3 tablespoons olive oil
1 clove garlic
¼ teaspoon ground cumin
⅛ teaspoon salt

1. If using canned garbanzo beans, drain and rinse beans.
2. Combine all ingredients in a food processor or blender. Process until smooth.

Tofu Avocado Spread

This creamy spread is rich in protein and potassium and pairs nicely with a piece of whole-grain toast.

INGREDIENTS | YIELDS ½ CUP

¼ cup firm tofu
½ ripe avocado
¼ teaspoon low-sodium soy sauce

1. In a small bowl, mash tofu and avocado.
2. Add soy sauce and combine well.

Is Your Avocado Ripe?

Hold the avocado in your hand and give it a soft squeeze. A nearly ripe avocado will yield slightly under the pressure. Avoid those that feel loose in their skin as these are overripe. If it feels like a stone, it isn't ripe yet.

Couscous with Grated Zucchini and Carrots

Butter or oil added to this dish prevents the couscous from forming clumps or curds. Remember that your baby needs fat for healthy brain and eye development.

INGREDIENTS | YIELDS 2 CUPS

1 cup whole-wheat couscous

1 cup water

2 tablespoons butter or canola oil

1 teaspoon flaxseed

½ cup grated zucchini

½ cup carrot rounds

½ teaspoon minced garlic

1 teaspoon olive oil

1 cup canned white beans

1. Add couscous, water, and butter or canola oil in a microwaveable glass bowl. Cover and heat on high for 2–3 minutes. Remove from microwave and fluff with fork. Sprinkle flaxseed on couscous and blend with fork.

2. Place zucchini and carrot rounds in a microwaveable bowl and steam until tender.

3. In a medium saucepan, sauté garlic in oil over medium heat until clear, about 3 minutes. Add beans, cooked zucchini, and carrots to the pan and heat through.

4. Combine couscous, beans, zucchini, and carrots.

How Do You Use Flaxseeds?

One way to use flaxseeds is to purchase fresh flaxseeds. Store them in the refrigerator and grind them right before use. Get an inexpensive coffee grinder that you use specifically for this purpose. Grind in small batches and store in an airtight container in the fridge. Use these quickly once they have been ground.

Hawaiian Sweet Potatoes

Roasting the sweet potatoes with the pineapple gives this dish a festive air without any added sugar.

INGREDIENTS | YIELDS 2 CUPS

1 large sweet potato
1 cup chopped pineapple

1. Preheat oven to 375°F.
2. Peel sweet potato and cut into wedges lengthwise. Arrange sweet potato wedges in a small baking dish. Cover sweet potatoes with pineapple pieces and juice.
3. Bake for 45–55 minutes, or until sweet potatoes are tender.

The World-Traveling Pineapple

Although pineapples are native to Paraguay and Brazil, they made their way around the world on sailing vessels. Sailors ate them to prevent scurvy. The same vitamin C that kept sailors healthy also helps keep today's little ones healthy.

Turkey Chili

If this chili is not spicy enough for the adults, add extra chili powder, green chilies, or serrano peppers to the adult portion and heat through.

INGREDIENTS | YIELDS 12 CUPS

2 tablespoons canola oil
1 medium red onion, chopped
1 clove garlic, minced
1 pound ground turkey breast
1 pound butternut squash, peeled, seeded, and cut into 1" cubes
½ cup vegetable broth
2 (14.5-ounce) cans petite diced tomatoes
1 (15-ounce) can black beans with liquid
1 (15.5-ounce) can white hominy, drained
1 (8-ounce) can tomato sauce
2 teaspoons chili powder
1 tablespoon ground cumin
⅛ teaspoon ground cinnamon
1 cup plain yogurt

1. In a large pot, heat the canola oil over medium heat. Add onion and garlic; cook and stir for 3 minutes until clear.

2. Add ground turkey. Stir until crumbly and no longer pink, about 5–7 minutes.

3. Add the butternut squash, broth, tomatoes, black beans, hominy, and tomato sauce; season with chili powder, cumin, and cinnamon.

4. Bring to a simmer, then reduce heat to medium-low, cover, and simmer until the squash is tender, about 20 minutes.

5. Top each bowl with 1–2 tablespoons of yogurt to serve.

Whole-Wheat Rotini
with Bolognese Sauce

In Italy, bowls of pasta are layered differently. The sauce is the most important part of the meal so the pasta is added to the sauce, instead of the sauce being added on top of the pasta.

INGREDIENTS | YIELDS 2 CUPS OF SAUCE

2 tablespoons olive oil
2 tablespoons butter or trans fat–free margarine
½ Vidalia onion, diced
½ stalk celery, diced
½ carrot, diced
1 pound lean ground beef
1 (15-ounce) can tomato sauce
2 tablespoons tomato paste
Whole-wheat rotini, cooked
Grated Parmesan cheese, for garnish

1. In a large pot, heat olive oil and butter over medium heat. Add onion, celery, and carrot and sauté until onion is clear, about 5–7 minutes.
2. Add ground beef and cook thoroughly, about 8–10 minutes.
3. Add tomato sauce and paste and heat through.
4. Mix whole-wheat rotini and sauce, top with Parmesan cheese, and serve.

Want to Have Lunch in Rome?

In Italy, lunch is the largest meal of the day. Breakfast is typically small, lunch often has many courses, and then dinner tends to be smaller portions of leftovers from lunch. Italian diets are rich in whole grains, vegetables, fish, and olive oil. This pattern of eating is often associated with low rates of heart disease.

Apple-Roasted Carrots

Cooked carrot slices make a great food for self-feeding. The rounds are just the right size for little fingers.

INGREDIENTS | YIELDS ½ CUP

4 medium carrots
¼ cup apple juice concentrate

1. Preheat oven to 450°F. Lightly oil a baking sheet.
2. Peel and thinly slice carrots.
3. Toss carrots with apple juice concentrate in a medium bowl.
4. Spread carrot slices on prepared baking sheet.
5. Bake 10–12 minutes, or until carrots are tender.

Orzo with Creamy Tomato Spinach Sauce

If using frozen spinach, thaw before using in this recipe.

INGREDIENTS | YIELDS 2½ CUPS

¾ cup orzo (or other very small pasta)

½ cup marinara sauce

¼ cup silken tofu

¼ cup chopped spinach

1. Cook orzo according to package directions. Drain and set aside.
2. In a food processor, combine pasta sauce, tofu, and spinach. Process until smooth.
3. Transfer sauce to a small saucepan over medium heat. Heat through.
4. Stir orzo into sauce.

Tofu, an Early Finger Food

When adults eat tofu, it is usually cooked; but cold tofu is a great early finger food for children. Cut firm or extra-firm tofu into small blocks for self-feeding.

Parsnip and Chicken Purée

Broth adds extra flavor to this dish, while providing the liquid necessary to attain the proper consistency.

INGREDIENTS | YIELDS ½ CUP

2 small parsnips
2 ounces boiled, shredded chicken
¼ cup vegetable or chicken broth

1. Peel parsnips and cut into small slices or chunks.
2. Steam parsnips using either a steamer basket or microwave.
3. In a blender or food processor, purée parsnips and chicken with broth.

Mango Honeydew Sorbet

Sweet honeydew and flavorful mango combine for an interesting frozen combination.

INGREDIENTS | YIELDS 4 CUPS

½ medium honeydew, cubed
1½ cups cubed mango
½ cup apple juice

1. In a food processor or blender, purée all ingredients together.
2. Pour into a freezer-safe container.
3. After 1½ –2 hours, fluff sorbet with a fork, then return to freezer.
4. After 2 hours, fluff sorbet with a fork.
5. Continue this process until ready to serve.

Strawberry Cantaloupe Sorbet

Since this frozen treat has no added sugar, it can be served as a healthy snack on a hot day, as well as a dessert.

INGREDIENTS | YIELDS 4 CUPS

½ medium cantaloupe, cubed
1½ cups sliced strawberries
½ cup apple juice

1. In a food processor or blender, purée all ingredients together. Pour into a freezer-safe container.

2. After 1½–2 hours, fluff sorbet with a fork, then return to freezer. After 2 more hours, fluff sorbet with a fork and return to freezer. Continue this process until ready to serve.

Pyrex Casserole Dishes Are Not Just for Baking

A covered Pyrex casserole with a shallow rectangle shape makes it easy to store sorbet in a crowded freezer and the easy-to-remove lids keep freezer odors out, while keeping liquid in. If Pyrex isn't available, a stainless steel mixing bowl covered with aluminum foil works well, too.

Sweet Potato Spread

Serve this sweet spread to add vitamins to graham crackers or whole grain toast.

INGREDIENTS | YIELDS 1 CUP

1 cup grated raw sweet potato
¾ cup water
1 teaspoon maple syrup
¼ teaspoon ground cinnamon
⅛ teaspoon ground nutmeg
2 tablespoons cream cheese

1. Bring sweet potato and water to a boil in a medium saucepan. Boil for 5 minutes.
2. Reduce heat to low and stir in remaining ingredients.
3. Keep stirring until cream cheese is melted and all ingredients are combined.

Blackberry Frozen Yogurt

Blueberries, raspberries, or strawberries can be substituted for blackberries in this recipe.

INGREDIENTS | YIELDS 1½ CUPS

½ cup frozen blackberries
1 tablespoon apple juice concentrate
1 cup vanilla yogurt (dairy or soy)

1. Blend all ingredients in a food processor or blender.
2. Transfer to a freezer-safe container. Freeze for 1 hour.
3. Remove from freezer and fluff with a fork.
4. Return to freezer, repeating process until ready to serve.

Strawberry Applesauce

*You can also make the Homemade Applesauce recipe in Chapter 4
and then add the strawberries.*

INGREDIENTS | YIELDS 2 CUPS

1 cup peeled and diced apples
1 cup sliced strawberries
¼ cup apple juice

1. In a medium saucepan, add all ingredients. Cover and simmer for about 10–15 minutes, until fruit is tender.

2. Mash with potato masher or purée in blender to desired consistency.

Apples and Carrots

Many fruits combined with apples will create wonderful "sauces." Try unique combinations of fruits and vegetables. For example, create a mixed-berry applesauce using blackberries and blueberries. Whip up an orange applesauce, or even try a carrot applesauce!

Happy Birthday Vanilla Cake

This birthday cake gets its sweetness from apple juice and maple syrup instead of from refined sugar.

INGREDIENTS | YIELDS 8" OR 9" CAKE

1 cup white, all-purpose flour

½ cup oat flour

2¼ teaspoons baking powder, divided

¼ teaspoon salt

¼ cup applesauce

½ cup apple juice concentrate

½ cup whole milk (dairy or soy)

¼ cup canola oil

¼ cup maple syrup

1½ teaspoons vanilla extract

1. Preheat oven to 375°F. Lightly oil an 8"–9" square or round cake pan.

2. In a medium mixing bowl, combine flours, 2 teaspoons baking powder, and salt.

3. In a large mixing bowl, combine applesauce with ¼ teaspoon baking powder. Add apple juice concentrate, milk, oil, syrup, and vanilla to the applesauce.

4. Mix ½ dry ingredients into wet until fully incorporated. Add remaining dry ingredients and mix well.

5. Pour batter into pan. Bake for 25 minutes, or until a toothpick inserted into the middle comes out clean.

Make Your Own Oat Flour

Making your own oat flour is easy. Just take old-fashioned rolled oats and blend them in the blender or food processor. Keep blending until you have a fine, powdery flour. Replacing a portion of white flour with oat flour will provide some whole-grain goodness to your dessert recipes.

Happy Birthday Carrot Cake

This extra-moist cake gets all of its sweetness from pineapple and maple syrup, rather than refined sugar.

INGREDIENTS | YIELDS 8" CAKE

1½ cups white whole-wheat flour

½ cup oat flour

2 teaspoons baking powder, divided

1 teaspoon baking soda

¼ teaspoon salt

1 cup canned crushed pineapple

¼ cup softened butter or trans-fat free margarine

½ cup maple syrup

1 teaspoon vanilla extract

2 medium carrots, peeled and grated

1. Preheat oven to 350°F.

2. In a medium bowl, combine flours, 1½ teaspoons baking powder, baking soda, and salt.

3. In a large bowl, combine pineapple purée with ½ teaspoon baking powder.

4. Add butter or margarine, maple syrup, and vanilla. Mix well with a wooden spoon.

5. Slowly mix dry ingredients into wet. Mix in grated carrots.

6. Scrape batter into a lightly oiled 8" baking pan.

7. Bake for 45–50 minutes, or until a toothpick inserted into the middle of the cake comes out clean.

Make Your Own Pineapple Purée

If you would prefer to use fresh pineapple instead of canned, crushed pineapple in this recipe, you can make your own purée. First, cut the ends off a fresh pineapple. Then, cut the pineapple in quarters. Cut off the tough outer skin, and cut out the fibrous core. Then, cut the pineapple in chunks, toss in the food processor, and purée.

Cream Cheese Frosting

This no-sugar-added frosting pairs very nicely with Happy Birthday Carrot Cake (see recipe in this chapter).

INGREDIENTS | YIELDS 1⅓ CUPS

1 cup cream cheese (dairy or soy)
⅓ cup pineapple purée or canned crushed pineapple
2 tablespoons apple juice concentrate

Using a blender or electric mixer, combine all ingredients.

Orange Coconut Sorbet

Sweet and creamy, this dessert adds important fat and vitamin C.

INGREDIENTS | YIELDS 3 CUPS

2 cups orange juice
1 cup light coconut milk
2 tablespoons agave nectar

1. In a medium bowl, combine juice and coconut milk.

2. Pour into a covered freezer-safe container.

3. After 1½ –2 hours, fluff with a fork, and return to freezer.

4. Continue freezing and fluffing until ready to serve.

Softening Sorbet

Sorbet can harden if left in the freezer overnight. Take sorbet out of the freezer and let sit on the counter for 5 minutes to allow it to soften before serving.

CHAPTER 6

Twelve to Eighteen Months

Broccoli Cheese Soup

This is a great soup on a cold winter day! Use frozen broccoli for convenience and if needed, this soup can be puréed to achieve the appropriate consistency for your toddler.

INGREDIENTS | YIELDS 8–9 CUPS

½ cup butter
7 tablespoons all-purpose flour
5 cups whole milk (dairy or soy), divided
2 vegetable bouillon cubes
2½ cups shredded Cheddar cheese, divided
1½ large bunches broccoli, florets finely chopped

1. In a large saucepan over medium heat, melt butter. Add flour to butter and stir to create a thick paste.

2. Add 2 cups milk and bouillon cubes. Reduce heat to low and cook until sauce begins to thicken, about 5–7 minutes.

3. Add 3 cups milk. Slowly add ½ cup Cheddar cheese, stirring to allow cheese to melt. Continue adding cheese ½ cup at a time until all the cheese has been added.

4. Add broccoli florets and allow to cook until tender, about 5–7 minutes.

Get Creative

The base of this soup can be used for many other soups. Get creative and add different combinations to the soup. Make a baked potato soup, a fish and potato soup, or a corn chowder soup. Soup bases come in handy in all types of cooking. Steps 1–2 of this recipe can be used to replace a can of condensed soup.

Cream of Potato Soup

Slow cookers can be an easy way to prepare meals for your infant or toddler. Assemble the ingredients in the morning and then forget about it until it's time for dinner!

INGREDIENTS | YIELDS 8–9 CUPS

6 medium russet potatoes, peeled and cubed

2 medium sweet onions, chopped

1 medium carrot, peeled and sliced

1 stalk celery, sliced

4 chicken bouillon cubes

1 tablespoon dried parsley flakes

5 cups water

⅓ cup butter

1 (12-ounce) can evaporated milk

Instant mashed potatoes (optional)

1. Combine all ingredients except evaporated milk in a 4-quart slow cooker.

2. Cover and cook on low for 10–12 hours or on high for 3–4 hours.

3. Stir in evaporated milk during the last hour.

4. Adjust the consistency of the soup by adding instant mashed potatoes, if needed.

Citrusy Rice Salad

*Keep the extra dressing in a separate container
to redress any leftover salad.*

INGREDIENTS | YIELDS 3 CUPS

¼ cup green beans
¼ cup chopped orange pieces
¼ cup pineapple chunks
2 green onions
2 cups cooked short-grain brown rice
¼ cup orange juice
1 teaspoon agave nectar
¼ cup olive oil

1. Steam green beans until tender. Plunge into cold water to stop cooking process.

2. Cut fruit and beans into bite-sized pieces.

3. Thinly slice white portion of green onions.

4. In a medium bowl, combine rice, chopped fruit, and vegetables.

5. In a jar with a tight-fitting lid, combine orange juice, agave nectar, and olive oil. Shake to combine.

6. Toss salad with dressing to taste.

Creamy Cauliflower Soup

For added texture, remove ⅓ of the soup before puréeing. After soup is puréed, return to pot and combine with reserved soup.

INGREDIENTS | YIELDS 6 CUPS

½ medium sweet onion, chopped
1 tablespoon olive oil
3 medium russet potatoes, peeled and diced
1 medium head cauliflower, chopped
4 cups vegetable broth
2 tablespoons nutritional yeast
½ teaspoon white pepper
½ teaspoon salt
1 bay leaf
1 cup plain yogurt (soy or dairy)

1. In a large stockpot over medium heat, sauté onion in olive oil.

2. Add remaining ingredients; bring to a boil.

3. Reduce heat to a simmer. Simmer approximately 30 minutes until potatoes and cauliflower are tender.

4. Remove bay leaf, move soup to a blender, and purée.

The White "Green" Vegetable

The saying "eat your green vegetables" should have the amendment—"and cauliflower." This late-season nutritional powerhouse is a cruciferous vegetable; it's in the same family as broccoli, cabbage, and kale. It has high levels of vitamin C and significant amounts of vitamin B_6, folate, and dietary fiber.

Chicken Salad

The consistency of this chicken salad will be better for your child closer to 18 months. Serve this on whole-wheat crackers or whole-wheat pita. Use this to stuff pea pods or celery as a fun snack for your children.

INGREDIENTS | YIELDS 1½ CUPS

1 (10-ounce) can white meat chicken, drained
2 tablespoons dried blueberries
¼ cup Vegenaise

In a medium bowl, combine all ingredients and mix well.

Mushroom Barley Casserole

Experiment with this dish by adding a green vegetable (e.g., broccoli, asparagus, or zucchini) before cooking.

INGREDIENTS | YIELDS 4½ CUPS

1 cup pearl barley
3 cups vegetable broth
¼ cup finely chopped sweet onion
1 cup chopped mushrooms (butter or cremini)

1. Preheat oven to 325°F.
2. Combine all ingredients in a covered 3-quart casserole dish.
3. Bake for 1½ hours.

Creamy Pasta Salad

This dressing works with many vegetables. Use your family's different combinations of favorite vegetables for this salad to mix up the variety in your diet. Try artichoke hearts, olives, broccoli, cauliflower, or summer squashes!

INGREDIENTS | YIELDS 4½ CUPS

Pasta Salad

3 cups cooked whole-wheat rotini
½ medium cucumber, peeled and diced
½ cup cooked carrot coins
½ cup sliced cherry tomatoes
4 ounces cooked chicken, chopped

Dressing

½ cup light mayonnaise or Vegenaise
¼ cup ranch dressing
3 tablespoons whole milk (dairy or soy)
2 tablespoons red wine vinegar
¼ teaspoon prepared yellow mustard

1. In a large bowl, combine pasta, cucumber, carrot coins, tomatoes, and chicken.

2. In a small bowl, combine all ingredients for the dressing.

3. Pour dressing over the pasta mixture and toss.

Quinoa Bean Salad

The key to successful quinoa is to thoroughly rinse your quinoa before you cook it. This rinsing helps the quinoa from becoming bitter tasting.

INGREDIENTS | YIELDS 6 CUPS

1 cup quinoa
2 cups water
1 (15-ounce) can of kidney beans
1 cup of frozen corn
1 medium red pepper, finely chopped
Juice of 1 medium lemon
⅓ cup finely chopped fresh cilantro
3 tablespoons balsamic vinegar
½ cup olive oil
2 teaspoons ground cumin
¼ teaspoon salt, or to taste

1. Rinse quinoa under cold running water until the water runs clear.

2. In a medium saucepan, place quinoa and water. Place on medium heat and cook for 10–15 minutes or until all the water is absorbed. Fluff with fork.

3. Combine quinoa with remaining ingredients in a large bowl. Mix thoroughly, chill, and serve.

Quinoa Is a Complete Protein

Protein is made up of tiny particles called amino acids. There are nine essential amino acids that our bodies need to obtain from food since our bodies do not make them. Quinoa contains all nine of these essential amino acids. As long as your family eats a variety of food, you should be getting enough protein without worrying about combining foods to make complete proteins.

Lemony Rice and Asparagus Salad

Save extra dressing for leftover rice salad. Overnight, the rice will absorb the dressing and will benefit from the extra flavor.

INGREDIENTS | YIELDS 4 CUPS

2 cups enriched white rice
4 cups water
1 bunch asparagus
¼ cup olive oil
½ cup lemon juice
2 tablespoons minced fresh dill

1. In a medium saucepan, bring rice and water to a boil.
2. Reduce heat, cover, and simmer 20 minutes, or until liquid is absorbed.
3. Let rice sit covered 5 minutes before fluffing with a fork.
4. While rice cooks, clean asparagus and remove tough ends. Chop asparagus into 1" pieces. Steam asparagus until bright and tender.
5. Combine olive oil and lemon juice in a lidded jar. Shake to combine.
6. Combine rice, asparagus, dill, and ½ cup of the dressing.
7. Chill before serving.

The Plant that Keeps on Giving

Asparagus, a perennial plant, is a member of the lily family. Asparagus spears are the shoots that grow from a crown that is planted approximately three feet underground. Although the shoots or spears are not picked for the first three years, the same plant can produce spears for fifteen to twenty years.

Zucchini Corn Muffins

Corn muffins get a boost of vitamins A and C from fresh zucchini in this tasty quick bread recipe.

INGREDIENTS | YIELDS 12 MUFFINS

1 cup cornmeal
1 cup white whole-wheat flour
2¼ teaspoons baking powder, divided
1 teaspoon baking soda
½ teaspoon salt
¼ cup applesauce
½ cup apple juice concentrate
¾ cup whole milk (dairy or soy)
3 tablespoons melted butter or trans fat–free margarine
1 cup grated zucchini

1. Preheat oven to 400°F.
2. In a medium bowl, combine cornmeal, flour, 2 teaspoons baking powder, baking soda, and salt.
3. In a large bowl, combine applesauce with ¼ teaspoon baking powder.
4. Add apple juice concentrate, milk, and melted butter or trans fat–free margarine to the applesauce.
5. Slowly mix dry ingredients into wet.
6. Mix the zucchini into the batter.
7. Spoon into oiled muffin pan.
8. Bake for 18–22 minutes, or until a toothpick inserted into the center of a muffin comes out clean.

Spicy Pumpkin Muffins

*These muffins are extremely moist and packed with
vitamin A, potassium, calcium, and fiber.*

INGREDIENTS | YIELDS 12 MUFFINS

2½ cups white whole-wheat flour
2¼ teaspoons baking powder, divided
¾ teaspoon salt
1½ teaspoons ground cinnamon
½ teaspoon ground nutmeg
¾ cup applesauce
¼ cup canola oil
¼ cup blackstrap molasses
½ cup agave nectar
1 teaspoon vanilla extract
2 cups cooked pumpkin (or 15-ounce can)

1. Preheat oven to 350°F. Lightly oil a standard muffin pan.

2. In a medium bowl, combine flour, 1½ teaspoons baking powder, salt, cinnamon, and nutmeg.

3. In a large bowl, combine applesauce with ¾ teaspoon baking powder.

4. Add oil, molasses, agave nectar, vanilla, and pumpkin to applesauce mixture. Stir to combine.

5. Slowly add dry ingredients to wet.

6. Spoon into muffin pan.

7. Bake for 25–30 minutes, or until a toothpick inserted into the center of a muffin comes out clean.

Corn Muffins

Serve these corn muffins as a breakfast treat or with a warm soup like Lentil Soup (see Chapter 5).

INGREDIENTS | YIELDS 12 MUFFINS

1 cup cornmeal

1 cup white whole-wheat flour

2¼ teaspoons baking powder, divided

1 teaspoon baking soda

¼ cup applesauce

½ cup agave nectar

1 cup whole milk (dairy or soy)

3 tablespoons canola oil

1. Preheat oven to 400°F. Lightly oil a standard muffin pan.
2. In a medium bowl, combine cornmeal, flour, 2 teaspoons of baking powder, and baking soda.
3. In a large bowl, combine applesauce and ¼ teaspoon baking powder.
4. Add agave nectar, milk, and oil to applesauce mixture.
5. Slowly mix dry ingredients into wet, being careful not to overstir.
6. Divide batter into muffin pan.
7. Bake for 25–30 minutes, or until a toothpick inserted into the center comes out clean.

As American As Cornbread?

Cornbread's history is tied to the history of the United States. Long before Europeans settled in the colonies of the New World, Native Americans were grinding corn into cornmeal. Upon arriving in their new home, the European settlers learned to make what is now known as cornbread.

Blueberry Pancakes

What weekend morning is complete without pancakes?
These pancakes are a nice break from pre-mixed
pancake mixes. They are healthful and taste great.
Try them with strawberries, bananas, or chocolate chips!

INGREDIENTS | YIELDS 15 PANCAKES (¼ CUP BATTER EACH)

1 cup whole-wheat pastry flour
2 tablespoons brown sugar
2 tablespoons baking powder
¼ teaspoon salt
1 tablespoon flaxseed meal
1½ cups old-fashioned oats
2 cups buttermilk
3 large eggs, beaten
¼ cup canola oil
1 pint fresh blueberries

1. Lightly oil a griddle and preheat to low-medium heat.

2. In large bowl, mix pastry flour, brown sugar, baking powder, salt, and flaxseed meal.

3. In separate bowl, mix old fashioned oats, and buttermilk. Then add beaten eggs and canola oil with a whisk until smooth and well blended.

4. Mix wet and dry ingredients together. Fold in blueberries.

5. Pour ¼ cup batter at a time onto the hot griddle. Cook until bubbles appear and then flip.

Fun Pancake Facts

Do you know how many times the person holding the world record for pancake flipping flip? The answer is: 416 times in 2 minutes! Do you celebrate pancake day? The official Pancake Day is the same day as Mardi Gras, or Fat Tuesday. It is the feast day before the start of the Lenten season of fasting.

Strawberry, Blueberry, and Banana Smoothie

This smoothie has a delightful purple hue.

INGREDIENTS | YIELDS 2¼ CUPS

½ cup frozen strawberries
½ cup frozen blueberries
½ frozen banana
½ cup apple juice
1 cup whole milk (dairy or soy)

Combine all ingredients in a blender. Blend until smooth.

French Toast

Make a large batch of these on the weekend and freeze. These are great frozen and then reheated in a toaster oven for an easy weekday breakfast. Serve with Blueberry Syrup in Chapter 5.

INGREDIENTS | YIELDS 8 SLICES

4 large eggs
2 tablespoons whole milk (dairy or soy)
¼ teaspoon ground cinnamon
½ teaspoon vanilla extract
8 slices whole-wheat bread

1. Lightly oil a griddle and preheat to medium heat.
2. In a medium bowl, combine eggs, milk, cinnamon, and vanilla.
3. Dip each slice of bread in egg mixture and place on griddle.
4. Cook until golden brown on each side.

Peach Raspberry Compote

Serve this compote with French Toast (see recipe in this chapter) or your favorite type of pancake.

INGREDIENTS | YIELDS 2 CUPS

1 cup chopped peaches

1 cup raspberries

2 tablespoons apple juice concentrate

Simmer all ingredients in a small saucepan until fruit starts to soften and break down, approximately 10 minutes.

What a Peach

The peach, a sweet, vitamin-rich summer fruit, is so delightful that Americans use its name to conjure up all kinds of positive images. From the complimentary, "She's a peach," to the upbeat, "I'm feeling peachy," the peach has become a synonym for sweetness. Although the nectarine is a smooth-skinned variety of peach, you just don't hear anyone saying, "You're such a nectarine!"

Cantaloupe Papaya Smoothie

This smoothie is a vibrant orange color.
It pleases the eyes as well as the taste buds.

INGREDIENTS | YIELDS 2¼ CUPS

1 cup frozen cantaloupe chunks
½ cup frozen papaya chunks
½ cup orange juice
1 cup milk (dairy or soy)

Combine all ingredients in a blender. Blend until smooth.

Maple Barley Breakfast

Cook a batch of barley and put it to use in several recipes, like this comforting breakfast or Italian Beans and Barley (see recipe in this chapter).

INGREDIENTS | YIELDS 1 CUP

½ cup whole milk (dairy or soy)
⅔ cup cooked pearl barley
1 tablespoon maple syrup

1. In a small saucepan over low heat, warm milk.
2. Top barley with warm milk and maple syrup.

Barley—A Fiber-Rich Grain

Although pearl barley is not a whole grain (the hull has been removed), it is still high in fiber. This is because dietary fiber is found throughout the barley grain. Barley can be a helpful digestive aid in children with constipation due to its high-fiber content.

Spinach Tomato Scramble

You can substitute chopped collard greens, kale, or other greens in this recipe to give your child's diet a greater variety of green vegetables.

INGREDIENTS | YIELDS 6 CUPS

3 large omega-3 fortified eggs
6 omega-3 fortified egg whites
¼ cup whole milk (dairy or soy)
1 teaspoon olive oil
½ cup spinach, chopped in food processor very fine
½ cup chopped tomatoes or mild salsa
½ cup shredded Swiss cheese (optional)

1. In a medium bowl, whisk together the eggs, egg whites, and milk.

2. Add 1 teaspoon olive oil to a medium skillet and heat on medium heat.

3. Once heated, pour egg mixture into pan and stir with spatula.

4. Mix in spinach and tomatoes or salsa.

5. Sprinkle with cheese, if desired.

6. Continue to stir and scramble until done. Remove from heat and serve.

Banana Yogurt Milkshake

Agave nectar or honey can be used to sweeten this to your taste.
Use different flavored yogurts to make different flavored milkshakes.
Blending crushed ice in the milkshake creates a thicker shake.

INGREDIENTS | YIELDS 2 CUPS

1 medium banana
1 tablespoon lemon juice
8 ounces vanilla yogurt (dairy or soy)
1 cup whole milk (dairy or soy)
1 tablespoon flaxseed meal

Combine all ingredients in a blender. Blend until smooth.

Milkshake Day

Want to celebrate your favorite milkshake? Who doesn't? You can start in June and finish in September. June 20 is National Milkshake Day. Go out and celebrate milkshake day as a family! Due to the popularity of chocolate milkshakes, they get their own separate holiday. September 12 is designated as National Chocolate Milkshake Day!

Orange Pineapple Smoothie

The combination of orange and pineapple is sure to bring a little sun (not to mention lots of vitamin C) into even the gloomiest day.

INGREDIENTS | YIELDS 2¼ CUPS

1 cup frozen pineapple chunks
½ frozen banana
¾ cup orange juice
¾ cup whole milk (dairy or soy)

Combine all ingredients in a blender. Blend until smooth.

Folic Acid for Your Next Baby

Women of childbearing age are strongly encouraged to consume 400 micrograms of folate or folic acid every day (this is the RDA for folate, a B vitamin). Folate is the form of the vitamin found naturally occurring in food, and folic acid is the form used to enrich foods like bread or breakfast cereal. Taking the RDA of folate/folic acid during pregnancy has been found to significantly reduce the incidence of neural tube birth defects. Since these defects usually occur before a woman even knows she is pregnant, it is important for any woman who could become pregnant to ensure that she is consuming the RDA for this important vitamin. Both oranges and orange juice are good sources of folate.

Baked Honey Pescado

This makes a very sweet fish. Adults may like it with the following modifications: no agave nectar and 2 ½ tablespoons of Dijon mustard. It is also great with a crusty loaf of bread topped with butter.

INGREDIENTS | YIELDS 3 CUPS

2 tablespoons wildflower honey
1 tablespoon light agave nectar
1½ tablespoons Dijon mustard
1½ tablespoons Vegenaise
1 teaspoon lemon juice
Sprinkle of salt
1 pound white sea bass

1. Preheat oven to 400°F.

2. In a small bowl, combine honey, agave nectar, Dijon mustard, Vegenaise, lemon juice, and sea salt.

3. Place fish in a lightly oiled shallow baking dish. Spread mixture on top of fish. Bake for 15 minutes or until fish flakes lightly with a fork.

Looking for White Sea Bass?

It often goes by a few different names such as kingcroaker, weakfish, or seatrout. It is a firm, whitish fish that has a mild flavor. This is a best choice for seafood as it is not overfished and is not at risk for mercury contamination.

Broccoli with Meat and Rigatoni

The meat in this dish can easily be omitted and the broth substituted with vegetable broth for a vegetarian dish. Another option would be to try this with protein crumbles as a meat substitute.

INGREDIENTS | YIELDS 8 CUPS

1 pound whole-wheat rigatoni pasta
½ pound lean ground beef
3 tablespoons olive oil
1 tablespoon butter
4 cloves garlic, minced
1 bunch broccoli departed into florets
1 cup free range chicken or beef broth
1 cup fresh basil, coarsely chopped, divided
Fresh chopped parsley, for garnish
Parmesan cheese, for garnish

1. Cook rigatoni pasta according to directions, drain, and set aside.

2. In medium pan over medium heat, brown ground beef. Drain and set aside.

3. In a large skillet, heat 3 tablespoons olive oil and butter. Sauté garlic until browned over medium heat. Add broccoli and stir gently until coated. Add broth and simmer until broccoli is al dente. (Al dente means that it is still slightly firm. This amount of broccoli should take about 8 minutes to become al dente.)

4. Add half the basil, drained rigatoni, and ground beef to skillet and mix thoroughly. Transfer to serving bowl, and top with remaining basil, parsley, and Parmesan cheese.

Honeyed Carrots

Carrots are loaded with vitamin A and E and
are great for babies and toddlers.

INGREDIENTS | YIELDS 2 CUPS

1 pound carrots cut into coins
1 tablespoon butter or trans fat–free margarine
2 tablespoons wildflower honey
1 tablespoon agave nectar
1 tablespoon lemon or lime juice
¼ teaspoon salt, or to taste

1. Steam carrot coins in the microwave until tender.

2. In medium saucepan, melt butter or margarine over medium heat.

3. In small bowl, combine honey, agave nectar, and lemon or lime juice.

4. Add carrots and honey mixture to saucepan with butter.

5. Heat through and mix until carrots are coated with honey mixture.

6. Remove with slotted spoon and serve. Sprinkle with salt to taste.

Chicken Pot Pie Muffins

Timesaver tip: Purchase a rotisserie chicken at your grocery store to use for the shredded chicken. This makes assembling this dish a snap.

INGREDIENTS | YIELDS 12 MUFFINS

1¾ cups chicken broth

¼ cup butter

4 cups whole-wheat croutons with garlic

1 packet dry ranch seasoning dip

1½ cups shredded chicken, cooked

1 cup frozen mixed vegetables (peas, carrots, green beans)

1 (8-ounce) can of white corn, drained

1 tablespoon wheat germ

1 tablespoon flaxseed meal

3 tablespoons water

3 large eggs

1½ cups shredded Cheddar cheese

1. Preheat oven to 375°F.

2. In a small saucepan, combine broth and butter and heat over medium heat until butter is melted.

3. In large mixing bowl, combine croutons and dry ranch packet. Then add chicken, mixed vegetables, corn, and wheat germ to bowl and mix well.

4. In a small bowl, mix flaxseed meal and water and allow to sit for 2–3 minutes. Add eggs and whisk with fork. Pour this mixture into large mixing bowl.

5. Pour butter and broth mixture into the large mixing bowl and mix ingredients together well.

6. Scoop mixture into muffin tins. Top each muffin with Cheddar cheese.

7. Bake for 18–20 minutes until done.

Arroz Verde con Frijoles Negro

*For a fun twist, serve this dish with warmed
whole-wheat tortillas instead of forks.*

INGREDIENTS | YIELDS 6 CUPS

5 cups vegetable broth, divided
1 bay leaf
2 cups short-grain brown rice
1 bunch spinach
2 tablespoons lemon juice
2 cloves garlic
2 cups canned black beans, rinsed and drained
¼ teaspoon black pepper, or to taste

1. In a large saucepan over medium-high heat, bring 4½ cups vegetable broth, bay leaf, and rice to a boil.

2. Reduce heat, cover, and simmer for 20 minutes.

3. While rice is cooking, thoroughly wash spinach and remove stems.

4. Combine spinach, lemon juice, and garlic in a food processor. Process into a paste, adding extra vegetable broth as necessary.

5. Remove bay leaf from rice and fluff with a fork. Stir in beans and spinach mixture. Add pepper to taste.

Macaroni and Cheese

Pasta comes in so many styles so it's perfectly acceptable to veer from the traditional elbow macaroni. Experiment with other fun shapes your child may like.

INGREDIENTS | YIELDS 10 CUPS

10 cups water
½ pound whole-wheat elbow macaroni
6 tablespoons butter
6 tablespoons all-purpose flour
3 cups whole milk (dairy or soy)
1½ cups grated mild Cheddar cheese
½ cup grated sharp Cheddar cheese
½ teaspoon salt
¼ teaspoon black pepper
⅛ teaspoon dry mustard

1. In a large pot, boil the 10 cups water. Add whole-wheat elbow macaroni and cook until tender. Drain and rinse well under cold running water.

2. In a large saucepan over medium heat, melt butter. Add flour and continue stirring until the mixture thickens. Add milk and continue to stir until this thickens up.

3. Remove from heat and add Cheddar cheeses, salt, pepper, and dry mustard. If needed, return to low heat and stir to melt cheese. Add cooked elbow macaroni and mix well. Serve.

Cheesy Grits

*Cheese grits are a traditional breakfast food
and side dish of the American South.*

INGREDIENTS | YIELDS 2¼ CUPS

½ cup grits
2 cups water
1 teaspoon butter or trans fat–free margarine
¼ cup shredded Cheddar cheese (dairy or soy)

1. In a small saucepan, combine grits, water, and butter or trans fat–free margarine. Bring to a boil, stirring constantly.

2. Reduce heat, cover, and simmer for 5 minutes.

3. Add grated cheese. Stir until cheese is melted.

Honored Grits

Grits, a dish made from ground, dried corn, was named the "Official Prepared Food" of Georgia in 2002. This honor marks the important place that this porridge has held in Southern cooking throughout American history.

Vegetable Tofu Pot Pie

Serve this warm, comforting dish with Strawberry Applesauce (see Chapter 5) for dessert.

INGREDIENTS | YIELDS 6 CUPS

2–3 large russet potatoes, peeled
2 medium carrots, peeled
1 small sweet onion
1 cup broccoli florets
4 large mushrooms (button or cremini)
2 tablespoons olive oil
1½ cups vegetable broth
1 tablespoon nutritional yeast
1 tablespoon garlic pepper
1 tablespoon poultry seasoning
1 teaspoon dried dill
1 tablespoon cornstarch
2 tablespoons cold water
½ pound extra-firm tofu
1 (9") frozen pie crust

1. Preheat oven to 350°F.

2. Chop all vegetables into bite-sized pieces.

3. Heat olive oil over medium-high heat in a medium skillet. Add potatoes, carrots, onion, and broccoli. Sauté for 3–5 minutes, until slightly soft. Add mushrooms and sauté for 1 more minute.

4. In a medium bowl, mix together broth, nutritional yeast, and spices.

5. Dilute cornstarch with cold water. Add to broth mixture.

6. Cut tofu into 1" cubes.

7. Toss cooked vegetables and tofu with sauce.

8. Pour into a 2–3-quart, round casserole dish. Add pie crust to top of casserole and pinch edges around top of dish. Prick pie crust with a fork.

9. Bake for 45–55 minutes, or until crust is golden and sauce is bubbling through holes in the crust.

Nutritional Yeast

Nutritional yeast is an inactive yeast that is grown on molasses. It is used as a flavoring agent and as a nutritional supplement, as it provides protein and B vitamins. Some nutritional yeast is enriched with vitamin B_{12}, a vitamin often lacking in the diets of vegetarians and vegans. Do not confuse inactive nutritional yeast with active yeast, such as baker's yeast. If consumed raw, active yeasts can continue to grow in the intestinal tract, robbing the body of essential nutrients.

Easy Baked Chicken

This is a simple but delicious recipe. The yogurt protects the chicken from becoming dry and gives it a nice flavor. This chicken is also a good base for adding your family's favorite seasoning. Mix the yogurt with barbecue sauce for a fun twist.

INGREDIENTS | YIELDS 4 CHICKEN BREASTS

1 pound boneless, skinless chicken breasts
1¼ cups full-fat plain Greek yogurt

1. Preheat oven to 350°F.
2. Coat chicken with yogurt and place in a medium baking dish.
3. Bake covered in aluminum foil for 10 minutes.
4. Remove foil and allow chicken to complete cooking uncovered for about 10 more minutes.

Greek Yogurt versus Regular Yogurt

Greek yogurt is known for its unique creamy texture. Greek yogurt is strained while still warm, which allows most of the whey to be removed. The end result is a thick and creamy yogurt that is high in protein, low in lactose, and tolerates heat well. Even the low-fat versions of Greek yogurt have the thick and creamy texture.

Homestyle Stuffing

This stuffing is a breeze to make.
Pair this with the Easy Baked Chicken in this chapter.

INGREDIENTS | YIELDS 12 MUFFINS

1¾ cups beef broth
¼ cup butter or trans fat–free margarine
4 cups whole-wheat croutons with garlic
1 packet dry stuffing seasoning mix
1 pound nitrate-free sausage, cooked and crumbled
1 cup carrots, steamed and diced
1 cup celery, steamed and diced
1 tablespoon wheat germ
1 tablespoon flaxseed meal
3 tablespoons water
3 large eggs
1½ cups shredded Cheddar cheese

1. Preheat oven to 375°F.

2. In a small saucepan, combine broth and butter or margarine and heat over medium heat until butter is melted.

3. In large mixing bowl, combine croutons and stuffing seasoning packet. Then add cooked nitrate-free sausage, steamed carrots, steamed celery, and wheat germ to bowl and mix well.

4. In a small bowl, mix flaxseed meal and water and allow to sit for 2–3 minutes. Add eggs and whisk with a fork. Pour this mixture into large mixing bowl with sausage.

5. Pour butter and broth mixture into large mixing bowl with sausage and mix ingredients together well.

6. Scoop mixture out into muffin tins. Top each muffin with Cheddar cheese.

7. Bake for 18–20 minutes until done.

Maple Acorn Squash

Cooking acorn squash in a water bath results in an extremely tender side dish.

INGREDIENTS | YIELDS 2 HALVES

1 medium acorn squash
2 tablespoons maple syrup

1. Preheat oven to 375°F.

2. Cut squash in half. Scoop out seeds and discard. Place squash, cut-side down, in a square baking pan. Fill with water until it is 1"–2" deep.

3. Bake for 45 minutes or until flesh is very tender. Pour out water, turn squash cut-side up, and pour 1 tablespoon maple syrup into each half.

4. Turn oven to broiler setting. Broil for 2 minutes.

Lentils and Brown Rice

Frozen carrot slices work well in this dish if fresh aren't available.

INGREDIENTS | YIELDS 3 CUPS

1 cup short-grain brown rice
2¼ cups water
2 medium carrots, peeled and thinly sliced
½ cup dried lentils
¼ teaspoon ground cumin
1 bouillon cube (vegetable, chicken, or beef)
1 tablespoon olive oil

1. Combine all ingredients in a medium saucepan. Bring to a boil.

2. Reduce heat, cover pan, and simmer on low heat for 40 minutes.

3. Turn off heat, let sit 5 minutes covered, then fluff and serve.

Turkey Divan Muffins

This is a great recipe for leftovers from Thanksgiving. It is an enjoyable way to use up your Thanksgiving turkey when people are tired of leftover sandwiches.

INGREDIENTS | YIELDS 12 MUFFINS

3 cups cooked brown rice
3 tablespoons wheat germ
2½ cups cooked turkey, shredded
¼ cup water chestnuts, diced
¼ cup white corn
2½ cups frozen broccoli
10 ounces cream of chicken soup
1¼ cups water
¼ teaspoon dry mustard
¾ cup shredded Cheddar cheese

1. Preheat oven to 400°F. Lightly oil a muffin tin.

2. Put ¼ cup cooked brown rice in the bottom of each muffin tin. Add ¼ teaspoon wheat germ to each muffin, on top of rice. Then add small amounts of turkey, water chestnuts, white corn, and frozen broccoli to each muffin.

3. In a medium bowl, combine soup, water, and dry mustard with a whisk. Pour into each muffin. Top each muffin with 1 tablespoon Cheddar cheese and bake for 15–20 minutes.

Spaghetti Squash with Italian Herbs

Spaghetti squash is also delicious when it is served with a tomato sauce, like the marinara sauce in Whole-Wheat Shells with Marinara Sauce (see Chapter 5)

INGREDIENTS | YIELDS 4–6 CUPS

1 medium spaghetti squash
2 tablespoons olive oil
1 clove garlic, minced
1 teaspoon dried basil
1 teaspoon dried oregano
¼ cup grated Parmesan cheese (optional)

1. Preheat oven to 350°F.

2. Pierce squash with a fork in several places. Place in a baking dish. Bake 1½ hours (1 hour for a small squash).

3. Cut in half and remove seeds. Scrape flesh with the tines of a fork to form spaghetti-like threads.

4. Heat olive oil in a skillet over medium heat. Add minced garlic and herbs. Cook 2 minutes or until garlic is golden, but not brown.

5. Toss "spaghetti" with oil and herbs. Top with Parmesan cheese if using.

Roasted Potato Salad

Roasting potatoes adds some variety to the traditional boiled potatoes that are usually used in potato salads. Roasting is an easy process that adds a nice, surprising flavor to your potato salad.

INGREDIENTS | YIELDS 4 CUPS

2 pounds new potatoes
¼ cup Herbs de Provence vinaigrette
½ red onion, chopped
¼ cup grated Parmesan cheese
½ teaspoon salt
¼ teaspoon black pepper

1. Cut potatoes into small bite-sized pieces and toss with vinaigrette.

2. Arrange on a baking sheet and put into cold oven.

3. Heat up oven to 450°F and roast potatoes for about 20–30 minutes. Turn potatoes about half way through the roasting process to allow even roasting.

4. Remove from oven and toss with remaining ingredients. Serve.

Vegetable Baked Risotto

This delicious dish delivers protein, iron,
fiber, and a variety of vitamins.

INGREDIENTS | YIELDS 4½ CUPS

1 cup Arborio rice
½ cup green beans
3 cups vegetable broth
1 cup broccoli florets
1 small zucchini, coarsely chopped
1 clove garlic, minced
1 cup cooked great northern beans
1 teaspoon dried basil
1 teaspoon dried oregano

1. Preheat oven to 325°F.

2. Rinse rice. Trim ends from green beans, cut into 1" pieces.

3. Combine all ingredients in a covered casserole dish.

4. Bake for 1 hour.

Creamed Spinach

Serve creamed spinach on a baked potato for a more filling dish.

INGREDIENTS | YIELDS 1½ CUPS

1 bunch spinach, washed and with stems removed
½ dinner roll or biscuit
2 tablespoons olive oil
1 clove garlic, minced
2 tablespoons white whole-wheat flour
½ teaspoon salt
¼ teaspoon black pepper
2–4 tablespoons whole milk (dairy or soy)

1. Roughly chop spinach. Wilt spinach in a dry skillet over medium heat.

2. Combine wilted spinach with the roll in a food processor. Process until finely chopped.

3. In a medium skillet, heat olive oil over medium heat. Sauté minced garlic in oil until fragrant.

4. Add flour, then salt and pepper. Add 2 tablespoons milk. Add spinach mixture. Add more milk until desired consistency.

5. Heat through and serve.

Italian Beans and Barley

For convenience, canned garbanzo beans and canned tomatoes work well in this recipe. Drain and rinse beans if using canned, but do not drain tomatoes.

INGREDIENTS | YIELDS 5 CUPS

2 tablespoons olive oil
1 clove garlic, minced
2 cups chopped green beans
2 cups cooked garbanzo beans
1 cup diced tomatoes
3 cups cooked pearl barley

1. In a large skillet, heat olive oil over medium heat.
2. Add minced garlic to olive oil. Cook for 2–3 minutes, until garlic is golden and fragrant.
3. Add green beans, and cook for another 5 minutes.
4. Add remaining ingredients, combine, and heat through.

Caribbean Baked Risotto

This dish is a complete meal incorporating fruit, vegetable, protein, and grain.

INGREDIENTS | YIELDS 4½ CUPS

1 cup Arborio rice

1 cup light coconut milk

3 cups vegetable broth

½ cup cooked pumpkin

1 cup pineapple pieces

½ cup cooked black beans

1 clove garlic, minced

1 cup chopped spinach

1. Preheat oven to 325°F.

2. Rinse rice. Combine all ingredients in a covered casserole dish. Bake for 1 hour.

Risotto

Risotto is a traditional Italian creamy rice dish. It is typically made by stirring a small amount of hot liquid, usually broth or stock, into Arborio rice until the liquid is absorbed. This process continues until all of the liquid has been absorbed and the rice is fully cooked with a creamy, starchy sauce. Baking Arborio rice brings about a similar result without standing in front of a stove for close to an hour, a luxury not many new parents can afford!

Creamy Salsa Dip

This dip makes snack time, fiesta time. Serve with Baked Tortilla Chips (see recipe in this chapter), Baked Pita Chips (see recipe in this chapter) or steamed veggies.

INGREDIENTS | YIELDS 2 TABLESPOONS

1 tablespoon cream cheese (dairy or soy)

1 tablespoon mild salsa

½ teaspoon agave nectar

Combine all ingredients in a small bowl and stir thoroughly.

Red Beans and Rice

Rice and beans are a staple food in many parts of the world. They go together because beans provide a protein that is lacking in amino acids, but is rounded out by serving it alongside nuts or grains, like rice, to make a complete protein.

INGREDIENTS | YIELDS 6 CUPS

2 teaspoons olive oil

1 (15-ounce) can kidney beans

1 cup marinara sauce

½ cup carrot purée

1 tablespoon wheat germ

½ teaspoon dried oregano

½ teaspoon dried basil

⅛ teaspoon dried thyme

¼ cup water

4 cups cooked brown rice

1. In medium saucepan over medium heat, heat olive oil.

2. Once hot, add beans, marinara sauce, carrot purée, wheat germ, oregano, basil, thyme, and water to saucepan and simmer on low heat until heated through.

3. Remove from heat. Mix with brown rice and serve.

When Do People Eat Red Beans and Rice?

Red beans and rice is a typical Louisiana Creole dish. This dish is traditionally served on Mondays. Why? It started as a way to use leftovers from Sunday night dinners. This version is not the traditional Creole red beans and rice, which might be too spicy for young toddlers. Feel free to spice it for adult members of the family with some added cayenne pepper or hot sauce.

Italian Eggplant

Whole-wheat pasta tossed with olive oil
makes a great complement to this entrée.

INGREDIENTS | YIELDS 8–10 CUPS

1 large eggplant
1 tablespoon salt
1 cup Italian-seasoned bread crumbs
2 tablespoons olive oil
3 cups marinara sauce (either homemade or jarred)
4 ounces shredded mozzarella cheese (dairy or soy)

1. Thinly slice eggplant. (The slicing attachment on a food processor works well for this.)

2. Sprinkle eggplant slices with salt, set aside for 20 minutes, then rinse.

3. Preheat oven to 350°F.

4. In a shallow dish, combine bread crumbs and olive oil. Toss eggplant slices in bread crumb mixture.

5. In a 9" × 13" casserole dish, alternate layers of sauce and eggplant, beginning and ending with sauce.

6. Top with mozzarella cheese.

7. Bake for 50–60 minutes, until cheese is melted and eggplant is tender when pierced with a fork.

To Peel or Not to Peel?

It is best to keep the skin on eggplant when cooking, as that is the part of the eggplant with the greatest amount of dietary fiber. To ensure that the skin will be tender upon cooking, use young, smaller eggplants rather than older eggplants, which might have tougher skin.

Mangosteen Cereal Mix

Mix it up! Use different types of cereals that are on hand. Different flavored fruit leathers and dried blueberries make a nice addition. Dried blueberries are small and are not a choking hazard like raisins or cranberries.

INGREDIENTS | YIELDS 8 CUPS

6 mangosteen fruit leathers
2 cups cinnamon whole-wheat cereal
2 cups corn cereal shaped in tiny balls
2 cups dried blueberries
¼ cup freeze-dried mango pieces

1. Cut fruit leathers into tiny bite-sized pieces.

2. Combine all ingredients in an airtight container.

What Are Mangosteens?

They are a tropical fruit and grow mostly in Southeast Asia. The rind of this fruit is purple and the inside fruit is white. This fruit is new to the arena of antioxidants but shows promise as being a good source of antioxidants. You can only find whole fresh mangosteens in Canada and Hawaii. Due to government regulations, only the juice can be imported to the United States, not the whole fruit.

Take-Along Cereal Snack

Since raisins can be a choking hazard for children under three, dehydrated fruits step in to create a tasty nutritious snack.

INGREDIENTS | YIELDS 4½ CUPS

3 cups O-type cereal
1 cup dried, diced apples
½ cup dried strawberry pieces

1. Combine all ingredients in a large bowl.

2. Store in an airtight container or bag.

Taking It on the Road

Cereal mixes, muffins, fruit-sweetened cookies, and dehydrated fruit are all great snacks to throw in baby's diaper bag for a nutritious snack. Children need to eat throughout the day and having a wholesome option on hand can contribute to a fun outing.

Vanilla Raspberry Sorbet

*For a seedless sorbet, press mixture through
a fine-mesh sieve before freezing.*

INGREDIENTS | YIELDS 2¼ CUPS

2 cups raspberries
1½ teaspoons vanilla extract
3 tablespoons apple juice concentrate

1. In a blender, combine all ingredients. Blend until smooth.

2. Pour into a freezer-safe container.

3. Freeze for 2 hours, then fluff with a fork.

4. Return to freezer.

5. Continue fluffing and freezing every 1½–2 hours until serving.

A Black-Belt in Good Health

Both raspberries and blackberries are rich with antioxidants. Antioxidants are believed to protect your body's cells from damage caused by tobacco, radiation, and even the unhealthy byproducts of food you eat.

Tropical Pudding Pie Dip

This tropical dip is a hit with kids! Serve this dip with an arrangement of in-season fruit to help your children try new fruits.

INGREDIENTS | YIELDS 3 CUPS

1 small package all natural instant vanilla pudding
1½ cups whole milk (dairy or soy)
1 cup light sour cream
⅓ cup orange-pineapple juice
½ teaspoon orange or lemon zest

In a medium mixing bowl, combine vanilla pudding and milk with a beater. Once blended well, add remaining ingredients and blend until smooth. Chill and serve.

Fruit Kabobs

Using plastic straws instead of sharp toothpicks or skewers makes this a safer treat for little fingers to manage.

INGREDIENTS | YIELDS 4 KABOBS

¼ cup 1" cantaloupe cubes
¼ cup 1" honeydew cubes
¼ cup 1" pineapple cubes
¼ cup 1" peach cubes
Small plastic straws (or drink stirrers)

Thread the fruit on the straws, alternating fruit pieces.

Have Fun with Food

Creating playful presentations can be fun for parents and children alike. Making smiley-face pancakes using artfully arranged blueberries or creating a flower out of fruit salad can make mealtime a happy time for everyone.

Sweet Sunflower Seed Butter Dip

*Serve this sweet dipping sauce with
cold steamed broccoli florets and carrots.*

INGREDIENTS | YIELDS 2 TABLESPOONS

1 tablespoon vanilla yogurt (dairy or soy)
1 tablespoon sunflower seed butter
1 teaspoon agave nectar

Combine all ingredients in a small bowl and stir well.

Pink Milk

*Why use mixes that are loaded with sugar and artificial colors and
flavors to give milk a fun boost, when the natural alternative is so easy?*

INGREDIENTS | YIELDS 2 CUPS

2 cups whole milk (dairy or soy)
¼ cup sliced strawberries

Combine all ingredients in a blender. Blend ingredients until
smooth.

Cinnamon Yogurt Fruit Dip

Children love to dip and this is a quick and easy yogurt dip that can be used with fruit or with vegetables. Using dips is a great way to increase your children's intake of healthy fruits and vegetables.

INGREDIENTS | YIELDS 1 CUP

1 cup vanilla yogurt (dairy or soy)
2 teaspoons wildflower honey or agave nectar
½ teaspoon ground cinnamon

1. In a medium bowl, combine and stir all ingredients until smooth.

2. Drizzle over fruit or use as a dip.

Cinnamon Is More than a Tasty Spice!

Researchers have shown that ½ teaspoon of cinnamon per day may help lower blood glucose in people with type 2 diabetes and may also help control cholesterol and improve brain function. Use cinnamon daily in your family meals or steep a cinnamon stick in teas or juice.

Baked Tortilla Chips

Use whole-wheat tortillas instead of corn for an interesting variation.

INGREDIENTS | YIELDS 40 CHIPS

5 corn tortillas
Sprinkle of sea salt
2 tablespoons canola oil put into spray pump

1. Preheat oven to 350°F. Spray a large cookie sheet with canola oil.

2. Cut tortillas into 8 wedges each.

3. Spread tortilla wedges on a cookie sheet in a single layer.

4. Spray tops of tortilla wedges with oil and sprinkle with salt.

5. Bake for 13–15 minutes until golden and crispy.

Some Snacking Ideas

Not every morsel that goes into your baby's mouth is likely to be homemade. There are some great organic snacks that can make being out and about with your baby a little easier. Here are some ideas: fruit cups, pretzels, dry cereal, and applesauce cups.

Baked Pita Chips

These make great chips for hummus. Serve these with the Hummus in Chapter 5 or with the Hummus Yogurt Dipping Sauce in this chapter.

INGREDIENTS | YIELDS 48 CHIPS

6 whole-wheat pita pockets
½ cup olive oil
½ teaspoon garlic salt

1. Preheat oven to 400°F.

2. Lay out 6 whole wheat pitas and brush both sides with olive oil.

3. Cut each whole-wheat pita pocket into 8 chips.

4. Sprinkle with garlic salt. Spread pita chips out on a baking sheet.

5. Bake for about 7 minutes or until pita turns brown and crispy.

Pita, Pita, Pita

Whole-wheat pita bread is a great base for many older baby meals. First, it is wonderful to use for dips. Second, it also makes a great pizza crust for making individual pizzas. Additionally, pitas can be made into pockets and can be used to stuff with sandwich fixings for a quick and healthy meal. When heating pitas, sprinkle both sides with water to prevent splitting.

Hummus Yogurt Dipping Sauce

This yogurt hummus tastes great when served with homemade Baked Pita Chips (see recipe in this chapter). You can also serve with fresh vegetables for dipping.

INGREDIENTS | YIELDS 2½ CUPS

1 (15-ounce) can garbanzo beans
1–2 cloves garlic, crushed
1 tablespoon lemon juice
½ cup plus 1 tablespoon plain Greek yogurt (dairy or soy)
1 teaspoon sea salt
½ teaspoon ground cumin

1. Drain can of beans and save liquid.

2. In a food processor, combine all ingredients and blend well.

3. Use reserved liquid from garbanzo beans to thin to desired consistency.

Moist Yogurt Pancakes

Pair these pancakes with Blueberry Syrup (see Chapter 5) for a breakfast sensation.

INGREDIENTS | YIELDS 20 SMALL PANCAKES

1½ cups unbleached all-purpose flour
½ cup oat flour
2½ teaspoons baking powder, divided
2 teaspoons baking soda
¼ teaspoon salt
½ cup applesauce
½ cup apple juice concentrate
2 cups plain yogurt (dairy or soy)
1 teaspoon vanilla extract
2 tablespoons butter or trans fat–free margarine, melted
Canola oil for pan

1. In a medium bowl, combine flours, 2 teaspoons baking powder, baking soda, and salt.

2. In a large bowl, combine applesauce with ½ teaspoon baking powder.

3. Add apple juice concentrate, yogurt, vanilla, and melted butter or trans fat–free margarine to the applesauce mixture.

4. Slowly stir dry ingredients into wet, stirring just to combine.

5. Brush skillet or griddle with oil and heat over medium-high heat. When a drop of water dances on the surface of the pan, drop batter onto surface.

6. When edges are golden and a couple of bubbles appear on the surface of the pancake, flip it and continue cooking on the other side.

7. Pancakes are ready when they are cooked through and golden on both sides.

CHAPTER 7

Eighteen Months and Beyond

Summer Barley Salad

The combination of steamed vegetable and sweet fruit brings a nice balance to this salad. You can substitute whatever is fresh at the farmers' market for this recipe.

INGREDIENTS | YIELDS 3 CUPS

½ cup green beans
2 green onions
½ cup strawberries, sliced
2 cups Basic Barley (see Chapter 4)
½ cup red wine vinaigrette (see sidebar)

1. Trim ends off green beans. Chop into 1" pieces and steam until tender.
2. Finely chop white portion of green onions.
3. Toss all ingredients in a medium bowl with the vinaigrette.
4. Chill before serving.

Red Wine Vinaigrette

Here is a simple recipe to make your own red wine vinaigrette. Combine the following ingredients in a tightly lidded jar: ¼ cup olive oil, ⅛ cup red wine vinegar, ⅛ cup lemon juice, and 1 tablespoon agave nectar. Shake before using.

Tofu Salad

Use this cool, summery salad as a filling for a pita pocket or tucked into a small melon half.

INGREDIENTS | YIELDS 3 CUPS

1 pound firm or extra-firm tofu
½ cup mayonnaise (regular or vegan)
2 tablespoons prepared yellow mustard
½ teaspoon dried dill
¼ minced sweet onion, like Vidalia
½ cup shredded carrot

1. Mash tofu with a fork in a medium bowl until crumbly.

2. Add remaining ingredients; stir to combine.

Tofu Storage

Store any leftover tofu in a sealed container. Fresh water should cover the tofu. Change the water every day, and the tofu should remain fresh for up to one week.

Cucumber Tomato Salad

Serve this dish as a topping to crusty fresh bread, or as a topping for fish or chicken. Consider giving your toddler a small bowl and some chips and allow her to "dip."

INGREDIENTS | YIELDS 4 CUPS

4 medium tomatoes

1 medium cucumber, peeled

½ red onion

1 tablespoon minced garlic

2 tablespoons extra-virgin olive oil

3 tablespoons red wine vinegar

¼ teaspoon each salt and black pepper, or to taste

1. Dice tomatoes, cucumber, and onion.

2. In large mixing bowl, combine all ingredients.

3. Add salt and pepper to taste.

Picking an Olive Oil Can Be Confusing

There are four descriptors that show the degree of processing in the olive oil. Extra-virgin olive oil means that this is the oil from the first pressing of the olives. Virgin olive oil is from the second pressing. Pure olive oil is then refined and filtered slightly. Extra-light oil has been highly refined and retains only a mild olive flavor.

Mango Coleslaw

The collard greens and coleslaw can be cooked for this recipe if your child is not ready to handle the crunchy texture of the raw vegetables.

INGREDIENTS | YIELDS 8 CUPS

3 stalks collard greens

5 cups shredded cabbage or bagged coleslaw mix

3 ripe mangos or 3 cups frozen mango

¼ cup red onion, chopped

2 tablespoons olive oil

1 tablespoon balsamic vinegar

1 tablespoon light agave nectar

1. Chop collard greens into tiny pieces.

2. In large mixing bowl, combine coleslaw mixture, collard greens, mango, and onion.

3. In small mixing bowl, combine olive oil, vinegar, and agave nectar and mix well to create dressing.

4. Pour dressing over contents in large mixing bowl.

5. Toss and serve.

Why Are Collard Greens Good for You?

Collard greens are excellent sources of vitamins K, A, and C. Furthermore, they are a good source of the nutrient manganese. What is manganese? It helps your body use the vitamin C in your diet. Manganese is also vital to the chemical properties that help create natural antioxidants in your body.

Tabouli Salad

The perfect summer salad. Make this salad at the peak of tomato season to use some of the best tomatoes produced all year.

INGREDIENTS | YIELDS 8 CUPS

3 cups quinoa, cooked
1 cup cannellini beans
1½ cups parsley, finely chopped
3 large tomatoes
3 green onions, sliced
1 tablespoon mint, finely chopped
¼ cup extra-virgin olive oil
¼ cup lemon juice

1. Combine all ingredients in a large bowl.

2. Chill for 2–3 hours and then serve.

Sweet Potato Biscuits

These easy-to-make little breads get a vitamin boost (and a nice golden color) from sweet potatoes.

INGREDIENTS | YIELDS 16 BISCUITS

½ cup applesauce
2½ teaspoons baking powder, divided
1 cup Sweet Potato Purée (see Chapter 3)
2 tablespoons olive oil
⅜ cup milk (dairy or soy)
3 cups white whole-wheat flour
1 teaspoon baking soda
½ teaspoon salt

1. Preheat oven to 425°F.

2. In a large bowl, combine applesauce with ½ teaspoon baking powder.

3. Add sweet potato, olive oil, and milk.

4. In a medium bowl, combine flour, 2 teaspoons baking powder, baking soda, and salt.

5. Slowly mix dry ingredients into wet.

6. Drop batter onto greased cookie sheet.

7. Bake for 10 minutes.

Traditional Potato Salad

Combining sweet potatoes and russet potatoes is a nice twist to a familiar dish.

INGREDIENTS | YIELDS 6 CUPS

4 large russet potatoes
2 medium sweet potatoes
3 large omega-3 fortified eggs
½ cup of sweet green peas
2 green onions, chopped
½ cup light mayonnaise or Vegenaise
1 tablespoon yellow mustard
¼ teaspoon each sea salt and black pepper, or to taste

1. In a large saucepan, boil potatoes until soft. Once soft, remove from heat and cut potatoes into bite-sized pieces.

2. In small pot, cover eggs with cold water and bring to boil. Cover and remove from heat for approximately 10 minutes. Remove from water, cool, and chop.

3. Place eggs and potatoes in a large mixing bowl.

4. Add peas, green onions, mayonnaise, and mustard and mix thoroughly.

5. Add salt and pepper to taste.

6. Refrigerate until ready to serve.

Are Sweet Potatoes Really Potatoes?

No! There are more than 100 varieties of edible potatoes but the sweet potato is not one of them. These two root vegetables are completely different. The potato's scientific name is *Solanum tuberosum* and its relatives are tomatoes, eggplants, and peppers. The sweet potato's scientific name is *Ipomoea batatas*, which is in the bindweed, or morning glory, family. Sweet potatoes are more closely related to flowers than they are to a regular potato.

Thumbprint Cookies

These cookies get their sweetness from fruit. Experiment with different flavors of fruit spread (e.g., strawberry, apricot, blueberry or plum).

INGREDIENTS | YIELDS 30 COOKIES

2 cups white whole-wheat flour
¼ teaspoon salt
¼ cup applesauce
¼ teaspoon baking powder
⅓ cup apple juice concentrate
2 tablespoons milk (dairy or soy)
⅔ cup butter or trans fat–free margarine, softened
1 teaspoon vanilla extract
½ cup all-fruit spread

1. Preheat oven to 350°F.

2. In a medium bowl, combine flour and salt.

3. In a large bowl, combine applesauce with baking powder.

4. Add apple juice concentrate, milk, butter or trans fat–free margarine, and vanilla to the applesauce mixture. Mix well.

5. Slowly add dry ingredients to wet. Stir to combine.

6. Form batter into 1" balls. Make a depression in the middle of each ball with thumb or back of a spoon. Fill depressions with fruit spread.

7. Bake for 10–12 minutes.

What Is White Whole-Wheat Flour?

White whole-wheat flour is a whole-grain flour made from an albino variety of wheat. Just like the browner whole-wheat flour, white whole-wheat flour is made from all parts of the grain, so it has the nutritional benefits of a whole grain. It has a sweeter taste than whole-wheat flour made from the red variety of wheat, and it is usually processed into a finer flour than traditional whole-wheat flour.

Raspberry Strawberry Muffins

Freeze any leftover muffins and reheat when needed.

INGREDIENTS | YIELDS 12 MUFFINS

2 cups white whole-wheat flour
1½ teaspoons baking powder, divided
½ teaspoon salt
½ cup applesauce
½ cup flaxseed meal
¼ cup canola oil
½ teaspoon vanilla extract
¾ cup maple syrup
¼ cup plain yogurt (dairy or soy)
¼ cup whole milk (dairy or soy)
¾ cup raspberries
¾ cup chopped strawberries

1. Preheat oven to 350°F.

2. In a medium bowl, combine flour, 1 teaspoon baking powder, and salt.

3. In a large bowl, combine applesauce with ½ teaspoon baking powder.

4. Add flaxseed meal, oil, vanilla, syrup, yogurt, and milk to the applesauce mixture. Combine well.

5. Slowly add dry ingredients to wet. Add raspberries and strawberries.

6. Spoon batter into lightly oiled muffin pan.

7. Bake for 25–30 minutes, or until a toothpick inserted into the center of a muffin comes out clean.

Breakfast Burrito

Purées and mashes are not just for babies. Use purées to boost the nutritional value of your family's meals. Adding a purée is an excellent method to increase the nutrient density of your meals and snacks without the battles.

INGREDIENTS | YIELDS 1 BURRITO

¼ cup Black Bean and Carrot Mash (see Chapter 5)
2 omega-3 fortified free-range eggs
1 tablespoon milk
¼ cup shredded cheese
1 whole-wheat tortilla
Salsa, for garnish

1. In medium saucepan, heat Black Bean and Carrot Mash until hot.

2. In a small bowl, combine eggs and milk and whisk with fork.

3. In a skillet, add egg mixture and cheese and cook over medium heat until done.

4. Spread tortilla with a thin layer of Black Bean and Carrot Mash; top with scrambled eggs and cheese mixture.

5. Roll up tortilla and top with salsa. Serve.

Barley with Bananas and Blueberries

Try barley for a breakfast cereal with different fruit combinations (e.g., strawberries, peaches, apricots).

INGREDIENTS | YIELDS 1¼ CUPS

⅔ cup cooked pearl barley
2 tablespoons blueberries
2 tablespoons banana slices
⅓ cup whole milk (dairy or soy)

Place barley in a small bowl, and top with fruit and milk.

Local Color

Fresh blueberries are a delight that can be found around the country at local farmers' markets from May to October. They grow in many regions of the United States and Canada, including the Northeast, the Eastern Seaboard, the Midwest, and the Pacific Northwest. Whether eating them freshly washed straight from the colander, mixing them into cereal or yogurt, or cooking them into a favorite recipe, these little blue darlings are sure to delight.

Egg and Cheese Strata

This is great to whip together the night before a family brunch or to have the morning after a sleepover party. Add some vegetables like roasted tomatoes, mushrooms, or spinach to boost the nutrition content of this dish.

INGREDIENTS | YIELDS A 9" PIE

6 slices whole-wheat bread
¼ cup butter
1 cup shredded Cheddar cheese
6 large omega-3 fortified free range eggs
1 cup whole milk (dairy or soy)
½ cup butternut squash purée
¼ teaspoon Dijon mustard

1. Butter slices of whole-wheat bread, cut into 1" cubes.

2. In medium bowl, combine bread and cheese and put into lightly greased pie pan.

3. Whisk together eggs, whole milk, butternut squash purée, and mustard. Pour egg mixture over bread and cheese. Cover and refrigerate overnight.

4. Bake at 375°F for 20–30 minutes or until top is brown and bubbly.

The Protein in Eggs Is Highly Bioavailable

What does that mean? The protein in eggs is easily and readily used by the human body for growth and development. It is the standard to which all other proteins are compared. In fact, 93.7 percent of the egg protein is used by the body, which is the highest of all protein sources. Eggs also contain all the essential amino acids, so they are a complete protein.

Sunflower Seed Butter and Banana Smoothie

For children who are going through a "picky" phase, this smoothie provides protein, calcium, and potassium in the guise of a treat.

INGREDIENTS | YIELDS 5 CUPS

1½ frozen bananas
⅓ cup sunflower seed butter
⅓ cup apple juice
2 cups whole milk (dairy or soy)
2 teaspoons agave nectar

1. Combine all ingredients in a blender.
2. Blend until smooth.

Sunflower Seeds—Not Just for the Birds

Sunflower seeds, the mainstay of many wild birdfeeders and baseball pitchers, are a great source of nutrition for your family. They are great sources of vitamin E and folate, plus a host of minerals. They are also a good source of protein and good fats. Grind some up into sunflower seed butter and add them to your recipes for a creamy, health-improving boost.

Blueberry and Banana Yogurt

Yogurt gets a nutrition and texture boost with the addition of fresh banana and crispy rice.

INGREDIENTS | YIELDS 2 CUPS

½ ripe banana
8 ounces blueberry yogurt
¼ cup crispy rice cereal

1. Mash banana in a small bowl.

2. Combine with blueberry yogurt.

3. Stir in crispy rice cereal.

Cherry Apple Coconut Rice Pudding

Since frozen cherries already have the pits removed, using them dramatically limits the prep time for this dish.

INGREDIENTS | YIELDS 4 CUPS

1 cup Arborio rice
1 (15-ounce) can light coconut milk
1 cup frozen cherries, thawed
1 cup chunky applesauce

1. Preheat oven to 325°F.

2. Rinse rice.

3. Combine all ingredients in a covered 2–3-quart casserole dish.

4. Bake for 1 hour.

Mixed Fruit Yogurt Smoothie

Feel free to substitute other fruits, such as honeydew, strawberries, or bananas.

INGREDIENTS | YIELDS 5 CUPS

1 cup frozen cantaloupe chunks

1 cup frozen pineapple pieces

1 cup frozen blueberries

1 cup vanilla yogurt (dairy or soy)

1 cup whole milk (dairy or soy)

1 cup apple juice

1. Combine all ingredients in a blender.
2. Blend well.

Nondairy Milk Alternatives

Not all young children are able to tolerate organic cow's milk. Fortunately, there are a number of nondairy milk alternatives available at well-stocked grocery stores. These are not meant to replace formula, but to be used in place of whole milk when an alternative is recommended. Look for vitamin-enriched milk alternatives. High-quality options include soy, rice, oat, or even hemp milk.

Roasted Winter Vegetables

This method works well for any root vegetable, including turnips, rutabagas, and beets.

INGREDIENTS | YIELDS 6 CUPS

1 large sweet potato
1 small butternut squash
2 medium parsnips
2 tablespoons olive oil
¼ teaspoon each salt and black pepper, or to taste

1. Preheat oven to 425°F.
2. Peel all vegetables and cut into chunks. (Remove seeds from squash before cutting.)
3. Toss in olive oil and salt and pepper, if using.
4. Spread in a single layer on a cookie sheet.
5. Bake until tender and sweet, approximately 20 minutes.

Barbecue Chicken Pizza

Prebaking the pizza crust helps this pizza not become soggy. If you make your own pizza crust from scratch or use a prepared dough, bake the crust first and then follow this recipe.

INGREDIENTS | YIELDS 1 LARGE PIZZA

3 tablespoons barbecue sauce
½ cup marinara sauce
1 prebaked whole-wheat pizza crust
8 ounces shredded cooked chicken
¾ cup shredded mozzarella cheese
¾ cup shredded Cheddar cheese
⅓ cup red onion, sliced thin
2 tablespoons chopped cilantro (optional)

1. Preheat oven to 425°F.

2. In small bowl, combine barbecue sauce and marinara sauce. Spread on prebaked pizza crust.

3. Top pizza with chicken, cheeses, and red onions. Bake for about 15 minutes.

4. Remove from oven, sprinkle with cilantro. Serve.

Chicken and Broccoli Stir-Fry

If broccoli is in season, use fresh organic vegetables. Combine broccoli, water chestnuts, baby corn, and red peppers and make your own stir-fry mix.

INGREDIENTS | YIELDS 8 CUPS

1 pound boneless, skinless chicken breasts

2 cloves garlic, minced

3 tablespoons honey

1 tablespoon light agave nectar

2 tablespoons low-sodium soy sauce

2 tablespoons orange juice

½ teaspoon fresh ginger, grated

⅛ teaspoon salt

⅛ teaspoon black pepper

1 package frozen broccoli stir-fry mix (broccoli, water chestnuts, peppers, corn)

2 teaspoons cornstarch

2 teaspoons cold water

4 cups cooked brown rice

1. Cut chicken into small strips.

2. Combine garlic, honey, agave nectar, soy sauce, orange juice, ginger, salt, and pepper in a medium bowl and marinate the chicken in this mixture for 1 hour.

3. In a large, lightly oiled skillet or wok, stir-fry chicken and marinade until chicken turns light brown. Remove from skillet but keep warm.

4. In same skillet, stir-fry the vegetables until heated through. Return chicken and marinade to pan.

5. In small bowl, combine cornstarch and cold water and mix until no lumps.

6. Place cornstarch in skillet with chicken and vegetables. Allow this to come to a boil and cook for 1–2 minutes or until thickened.

7. Serve over brown rice.

The Origin of Stir-Frying

In China, the origin of stir-frying had nothing to do with healthful cooking. It developed during a period of time in China when cooking materials and food were in short supply. Items had to be cooked fast without wasting any food and with minimum fuel. Now we know it is a healthful way to cook vegetables and preserve their nutrients.

Mixed-Vegetable Stir-Fry

For a heartier dish, add 1 cup of the protein of your choice (chicken strips, beef strips, or tofu) and serve over brown rice.

INGREDIENTS | YIELDS 5 CUPS

1 cup broth (vegetable, chicken, or beef)
1 tablespoon rice vinegar
1½ teaspoons low-sodium soy sauce
1 tablespoon cornstarch
2 tablespoons cold water
1–2 tablespoons canola oil
2 cloves garlic, minced
1¼" piece ginger, minced
2 medium carrots, chopped
½ red onion, chopped
2 cups broccoli florets
1 cup bok choy, chopped
1 cup cabbage, chopped

1. In a small bowl, combine broth, vinegar, and soy sauce.

2. Dilute cornstarch in cold water and add to broth mixture.

3. In a wok or large frying pan, heat oil over high heat.

4. Add garlic and ginger, and cook for 30 seconds.

5. Add carrots, onion, and broccoli. Cook for 2 minutes.

6. Add bok choy and cabbage. Cook for 1 minute.

7. Add assembled sauce and cook for 2 minutes. Cook until vegetables are tender, but not mushy.

Chicken and Udon Noodles

The spices in this dish can vary. In many areas of the world, baby food is spicy and children accept and tolerate spicy foods.

INGREDIENTS | YIELDS 6 CUPS

1 pound boneless, skinless chicken breasts

1 cup teriyaki sauce

1 (12-ounce) can crushed pineapple in natural juices

8 cups water

1 (9-ounce) package udon noodles

¾ cup sunflower nut butter

½ cup light coconut milk

½ cup vegetable or chicken broth

2¼ tablespoons carrot purée

2 teaspoons minced garlic

½ teaspoon ground ginger

2 tablespoons fresh lime juice

⅛ teaspoon red pepper flakes (optional)

1. Preheat oven to 350°F.

2. Arrange chicken in 9" × 13" baking dish and pour in teriyaki sauce and juice from crushed pineapple. Bake until chicken's internal temperature reaches 170°F.

3. In large pot, boil the 8 cups of water. Once boiling, place udon noodles in water and boil until tender, approximately 8–10 minutes. Drain noodles and rinse with cold water.

4. Blend sunflower nut butter, coconut milk, broth, carrot purée, garlic, ginger, and lime juice in blender until smooth. Use extra broth to thin to desired consistency.

5. Return noodles to cooking pot and pour content of blender onto noodles and stir to combine.

6. Cut or shred chicken into age-appropriate pieces for your child, and top with crushed pineapple and red pepper flakes if using. Serve with a side of the udon noodles and sauce.

Frosted Cauliflower

*For a more striking presentation, this can be made with the whole
head intact and then divided into florets when serving.*

INGREDIENTS | YIELDS 3 CUPS

1 head cauliflower
¼ cup plain yogurt (dairy or soy)
2 tablespoons prepared yellow mustard
1 teaspoon agave nectar
½ cup shredded Cheddar cheese (dairy or soy)

1. Preheat oven to 350°F. Bring a large pot of water to a boil.

2. Cut cauliflower into florets.

3. Drop florets into boiling water and cook for 1–2 minutes.
   Drain and rinse under cold water.

4. In a small bowl, mix together yogurt, mustard, and agave
   nectar.

5. Toss cauliflower in sauce.

6. Transfer to 1½-quart casserole dish; cover with cheese.

7. Bake, uncovered, for 20–25 minutes, or until cheese is
   melted.

Using Convenience Foods

With the increased interest in organic foods, a number of organic convenience foods have become available at well-stocked grocery stores.
Make these foods even more nutritious by adding a personal touch.
For example, you could add steamed cauliflower or broccoli florets to
macaroni and cheese, add colorful bell pepper rings to a frozen cheese
pizza, or top frozen waffles with fresh fruit and vanilla yogurt.

Roasted Carrots

Careful preparation is needed in this dish to ensure that your children are not at risk for choking. Cut each grape into quarters. Roast the carrots so that they are soft and easily chewed by your toddler. Cut them into pieces that are smaller than the windpipe.

INGREDIENTS | YIELDS 1½ POUNDS

8 ounces baby carrots, cut into thirds
1 tablespoon butter or trans fat–free margarine, melted
⅛ teaspoon ground cinnamon
1 tablespoon agave nectar
1 pound red seedless grapes, cut in quarters
1 medium pear, sliced

1. Preheat oven to 450°F.

2. In the microwave, steam carrots until slightly tender.

3. In a separate bowl, melt butter and combine with cinnamon and agave nectar.

4. In a medium bowl combine all ingredients together.

5. Spread mixture out on a baking sheet and roast in oven for 10–15 minutes or until tender.

Roasting Fruit in the Oven?

Roasting fruit is a wonderful way to bring out its sweetness. Winter fruits tend to roast better than summer fruits. Pears, apples, and oranges all roast wonderfully. Lightly toss them with olive oil and a little sea salt and roast them in a 450°F–500°F oven for about 15 minutes to bring out their roasted taste.

Pumpkin Risotto

This colorful dish makes a lovely meal when paired with a green salad or green vegetable.

INGREDIENTS | YIELDS 5 CUPS

1 tablespoon olive oil
1 tablespoon butter or trans fat–free margarine
1 tablespoon fresh sage
1 garlic clove, minced
¼ cup chopped sweet onion
1 cup Arborio rice
1 cup canned pumpkin
3 cups vegetable broth

1. Preheat oven to 350°F.
2. In a small skillet, heat olive oil and butter or trans fat–free margarine over medium-high heat.
3. When oil mixture is sizzling, add sage and minced garlic. Sauté for 1 minute.
4. Transfer herb mixture to a 3-quart casserole dish.
5. Add remaining ingredients, stir, and cover.
6. Bake for 1 hour. Stir before serving.

Pumpkins

There are many different varieties of pumpkins—and the ones you carve on Halloween won't taste particularly good! Look for the ones called "cooking pumpkins," "pie pumpkins," or some other designation that indicates they are meant to be eaten, not carved.

Quinoa Primavera

This dish is easy to vary according to your family's tastes. You can make it with many different vegetables. Vary the produce options depending on the season for freshest flavor.

INGREDIENTS | YIELDS 8 CUPS

1½ cups rinsed quinoa
3 cups water
1 cup frozen corn, thawed
1 medium red pepper, finely chopped
1 medium green pepper, finely chopped
1 medium cucumber, finely chopped
Juice of 1 large lemon
3 tablespoons flaxseed oil
3 tablespoons olive oil
3 tablespoons rice wine vinegar
¼ teaspoon salt, or to taste

1. Place quinoa and water in a medium saucepan. Turn on medium heat and cook for 10–15 minutes or until all the water is absorbed. Fluff with fork.

2. Combine quinoa with remaining ingredients in a large bowl. Mix thoroughly, chill, and serve.

What Is Rice Wine Vinegar?

Rice wine vinegar is popular light vinegar that is widely used in Asian cuisine. It is a vinegar made from rice wine and has a mellow and slightly sweet flavor. It is a nice addition to any marinade or vinaigrette dressing, or you can drizzle it over fish before cooking to give a light flavor.

Hummus and Mango Sandwich

*This creamy, sweet sandwich provides protein,
fiber, iron, and vitamins A and C.*

INGREDIENTS | YIELDS 2 MINI SANDWICHES

1 piece of whole-grain bread
1 tablespoon Hummus (see Chapter 5)
¼ cup mango slices

1. Spread hummus over the surface of the bread, and cut bread in half.

2. Top one half with mango slices.

3. Cover with other half of bread.

4. Cut sandwich into 2 pieces.

How to Choose a Mango

When selecting a mango, two senses come into play to determine which fruit is best. First, smell the mango at the stem end. It should have a nice fruity aroma. Second, touch the mango. It should feel firm, yet yield to gentle pressure in the same way as a peach.

Pinto Bean Roll-Ups

Serve these sandwiches with Creamy Salsa Dip (see Chapter 6).

INGREDIENTS | YIELDS 3 (2") ROLL-UPS

2 tablespoons Refried Pinto Beans (see Chapter 4)
1 whole-wheat tortilla
2 tablespoons shredded carrots
2 tablespoons shredded cabbage

1. Spread pinto bean purée over the surface of the tortilla.

2. Sprinkle on carrots and cabbage.

3. Tightly roll tortilla into a tube.

4. Cut tortilla tube into 3 pieces.

Grilled Cheese with Squash and Corn Purée

This recipe is a creative way to sneak vegetables into a child who might be picky about eating certain vegetables. Offer some corn or squash on the side of this so your child is exposed to a variety of fruits and vegetables.

INGREDIENTS | YIELDS 1 SANDWICH

2 slices whole-grain bread
1 tablespoon olive oil, butter, or trans fat–free margarine
¼ cup Butternut Squash and Corn Purée (see Chapter 4)
¼ cup shredded Mexican-flavored cheese
1 slice provolone cheese

1. Spread the outside of both pieces of bread with olive oil, butter, or trans fat–free spread.

2. Heat a medium skillet over medium heat.

3. Spread ⅛ cup of Butternut Squash and Corn Purée on the inside of one slice of bread and put in skillet.

4. Top with shredded Mexican-flavored cheese.

5. Add slice of provolone cheese.

6. Top sandwich with remaining piece of bread, coated with ⅛ cup Butternut Squash and Corn Purée on the inside.

7. Turn sandwich once. Heat in skillet until cheese is melted.

8. Remove from heat and serve.

One Squash, Two Squash, Three Squash, Four

Summer squashes are thinner squashes that bruise more easily. Winter squashes are more hearty and thick skinned. Both of these are excellent sources of nutrients. Squash is also a good source of calcium!

Pork and Beans

This can also be used as a side dish. Serve this recipe with the Mango Coleslaw found in this chapter.

INGREDIENTS | YIELDS 6 CUPS

2 pounds boneless pork ribs
14 ounces beef broth
1 (15-ounce) can black beans, drained
¾ cup mild barbecue sauce, divided
Whole-wheat rolls

1. In slow cooker, place pork ribs and beef broth. Cook on high for about 4 hours.

2. Once done, remove pork from cooker and shred it.

3. In small saucepan over medium heat, heat black beans until heated through.

4. Mix pork with 6 ounces barbecue sauce and black beans.

5. Serve on whole-wheat rolls and top with desired amount of barbecue sauce.

There's More to Pork and Beans

Pork and beans does not have to be chopped hot dogs and pinto beans. Adding spices and vegetables such as roasted red peppers, tomatoes, green peppers, and onions can also give your pulled pork a little kick. This pulled pork–and-bean mixture can also be wrapped in corn tortillas and topped with shredded cabbage to make a nice pork taco.

Bean and Avocado Quesadilla

Many of the infant purées can be added to quesadillas. Try a butternut squash and pinto bean quesadillas or a pumpkin black bean quesadilla . . . be creative!

INGREDIENTS | YIELDS 1 QUESADILLA

2 whole-wheat tortillas
½ cup Black Bean and Carrot Mash (see Chapter 5)
1 ripe medium avocado
¼ cup shredded Cheddar cheese
1 teaspoon canola oil
Salsa, for garnish

1. Spread 1 tortilla with a thin layer of Black Bean and Carrot Mash.

2. Cut avocado in half and scrape out the flesh into a small bowl. Mash avocado flesh with a fork.

3. Add avocado mash on top of black bean layer on the tortilla.

4. Sprinkle cheese on top of this layer and top with second tortilla.

5. In medium saucepan, heat canola oil on medium. Place quesadilla in skillet. Heat until cheese begins to melt. Flip and cook to golden brown. Remove from heat and cut into 8 triangles.

6. Top with desired amount of salsa. Serve.

Black Bean Roll-Ups

This is a great meal for fast weeknight dinners. The combination of beans, carrots, whole grains, and healthy fats provides a quick and balanced meal. Serve with some fresh fruit on the side.

INGREDIENTS | YIELDS 16 SPIRALS

1 teaspoon olive oil
¼ cup sweet onion, minced
1 teaspoon minced garlic
1 (15-ounce) can of black beans, drained and rinsed
½ cup carrot purée
1 teaspoon ground cumin
4 whole-wheat tortillas
¼ cup Avocado Mash (see Chapter 3)

1. Heat olive oil in skillet over medium–high heat.

2. Add onion and garlic to skillet and sauté until clear.

3. Add black beans, carrot purée, and cumin to the skillet.

4. Mash with potato masher until reach desired consistency. Cook until heated, about 10 minutes, and remove from heat.

5. Heat tortillas in the microwave for 30 seconds on high to warm.

6. Top one tortilla with a thin layer of bean spread and then Avocado Mash. Repeat with second tortilla.

7. Roll each tortilla. Cut each tortilla into 4 pieces.

Birthday or Sleepover Party Food

Spirals or roll-ups are typically a hit with children. You can make several different types of roll-ups and cut them into bite-sized pieces. Arrange them on a plate and let your child and their friends dig in. Children may be more willing to try new foods when they see other children try them. Peer pressure in reverse!

Cheesy Polenta with Roasted Vegetables

Combining the creamy polenta with the tender roasted vegetables yields a comforting stew.

INGREDIENTS | YIELDS 5 CUPS

2 medium carrots
4 asparagus spears
6 mushrooms (button or cremini)
2 tablespoons olive oil
⅛ teaspoon salt
3 cups water
1 cup polenta
½ cup shredded Cheddar cheese (dairy or soy)

1. Preheat oven to 425°F.
2. Peel carrots and cut into ¼"-wide matchsticks.
3. Break off ends of asparagus, and cut into 1"-long pieces.
4. Cut mushrooms in half.
5. Toss vegetables in olive oil and salt. Spread on baking sheet and cook until tender, approximately 10–15 minutes.
6. Bring water to a boil in a medium saucepan. Slowly whisk in polenta and keep whisking until polenta thickens and pulls away from the sides of the pan. Sprinkle on cheese, and stir to melt. In a large bowl, stir to combine polenta and vegetables.

Polenta, the Pasta of Northern Italy

Although Italy is known as the home of pasta and pizza, corn polenta has been a basic food item there since the late fifteenth century. Because corn, introduced to Italy from the New World, grows most easily in Northern Italy, polenta quickly became a culinary mainstay. It continues to be a very important component of Northern Italian cooking.

Black Bean Cakes

Serve these black bean cakes with
Spinach Tomato Scramble (see Chapter 6).

INGREDIENTS | YIELDS 6 CAKES

2 cups cooked black beans (or 1 [15-ounce] can)
3 tablespoons mild salsa
2 tablespoons bread crumbs
1 tablespoon canola oil

1. Drain and rinse black beans. Place in a medium bowl and mash beans with a potato masher or fork.
2. Combine mashed beans with salsa and bread crumbs. Form mixture into small cakes.
3. In a medium skillet, heat oil over medium–high heat.
4. Cook cakes on each side, approximately 2–3 minutes per side.

Broiled Pineapple with Frozen Yogurt

This "dessert" provides protein, calcium, and vitamin C.

INGREDIENTS | YIELDS 2 CUPS

1 cup vanilla yogurt (dairy or soy)
1 cup pineapple chunks

1. Transfer yogurt to a freezer-safe container.
2. Freeze for 1 hour, stir, and return to freezer.
3. Preheat oven to broiler setting.
4. Place pineapple on a baking sheet and broil pineapple until slightly browned, approximately 10 minutes.
5. Serve broiled pineapple topped with vanilla frozen yogurt.

Pineapple Salsa

Grilled pineapple can make a nice addition to this salsa. Cut a fresh pineapple in to ½" thick slices. Place on medium–hot grill and grill for 5–7 minutes per side. Allow to cool before using in cold salsa dish.

INGREDIENTS | YIELDS 4 CUPS

1 cup diced fresh pineapple
½ cup red bell pepper, diced
½ cup yellow bell pepper, diced
½ cup black beans, drained and rinsed
¼ cup red onion, diced
¼ cup cilantro, finely chopped
¼ cup orange-pineapple juice
2 tablespoons lime juice
¼ teaspoon each salt and black pepper, or to taste

1. In a large bowl, combine pineapple, red and yellow peppers, black beans, red onion, and cilantro, and mix well.

2. In a small bowl, combine orange-pineapple juice and lime juice. Pour into large bowl with pineapple.

3. Mix all ingredients together, season with salt and pepper to taste.

Orange Beets

How to boil your own beets: First, cut away the tops and 1" of the stem. Wash the beets but do not peel them. Place in a pot of boiling water and cook for 1½–2 hours. The skins slip off easily when done.

INGREDIENTS | YIELDS 4 CUPS

1 (8-ounce) package peeled and steamed ready-to-eat baby beets

1 (11-ounce) can mandarin oranges

1 fresh apple, cut into slices

¼ cup canola oil

3 tablespoons orange juice

1 tablespoon lemon juice

1 teaspoon orange zest

1. Cut beets into small slices.

2. In a large mixing bowl, combine beets with mandarin oranges and apple slices.

3. In a small bowl, combine oil, orange juice, lemon juice, and orange zest.

4. Toss dressing over fruit and chill. Serve.

Beets Not Your Child's Favorite Food?

It can take a while for your child to develop a taste for beets. Beets have one of the highest natural sugar contents of any vegetable, so they are great for roasting. Try roasting beets to bring out a sweeter flavor that might tempt your child. You can also try canned beets.

Potato Smash Up

You can also leave the skin on the russet potatoes for a different texture in this dish. Both russet and new potatoes taste nice with the skin on. Sweet potato skin, however, does not usually taste good in recipes.

INGREDIENTS | YIELDS 6 CUPS

2 medium sweet potatoes
2 medium russet potatoes
1½ cups cubed butternut squash
¼ cup butter or trans fat–free margarine
½–1 cup whole milk (dairy or soy)

1. Peel potatoes and cut into cubes of about the same size as the squash. Usually 1–2" cubes work the best.

2. Bring a large pot of water to a boil. Place potatoes and squash in boiling water and boil for about 20 minutes.

3. Drain potatoes and squash and place in a large mixing bowl.

4. Add butter and smash with a potato masher or hand mixer.

5. Add milk to reach desired texture.

Barbecue Meatloaf Muffins

Meatloaf without an egg? That's right, the flaxseed meal and water will thicken after 2–3 minutes and act as an egg replacer in this recipe.

INGREDIENTS | YIELDS 12 MUFFINS

1 tablespoon flaxseed meal
3 tablespoons water
1½ pounds extra-lean ground beef
1 cup tomato juice
¾ cup rolled oats
¼ cup chopped sweet onion
2 cloves garlic, minced
2 tablespoons chopped fresh oregano
1½ cups barbecue sauce

1. In a small bowl, mix flaxseed meal and water. Stir and allow to sit for 2–3 minutes.

2. Preheat oven to 350°F.

3. In a large bowl, combine beef, tomato juice, rolled oats, onion, garlic, and oregano. Add flaxseed mixture to the beef mixture and knead until well mixed.

4. Portion out mixture into a 12-cup muffin pan. Top each muffin with 2 tablespoons barbecue sauce.

5. Bake until muffins reach an internal temperature of 160°F.

Flaxseed Meal Can Replace Eggs

Flaxseed meal can be used to replace the egg that is traditionally used in meatloaf. Flaxseed meal is a source of omega-3 fatty acids, which are often lacking in the American diet. There is evidence to show that flaxseed is good for improving overall general health and preventing diseases.

Creamy Spinach Pita Pizza

Creamed spinach takes the place of traditional pizza sauce in this alternative Italian-style pie.

INGREDIENTS | YIELDS 1 PIZZA

¼ cup Creamed Spinach (see Chapter 6)
1 whole-grain pita bread
2 slices tomato
1 tablespoon grated Parmesan cheese (optional)

1. Spread spinach on surface of pita.

2. Top with tomato.

3. Sprinkle on Parmesan, if using.

4. Broil for 2 minutes; watch to prevent burning.

Pizza Crust Ideas

When it comes to pizza crust, don't feel like you have to stick to the traditional method of preparing your own dough. Consider these alternative ideas to form the base of a pizza: pita bread, English muffin, prepared pizza crust, tortilla, or a whole-grain waffle. With a little imagination, a pizza party is always possible.

Chicken Enchiladas

Using cream of chicken soup in place of enchilada sauce is a simple way to keep the heat down.

INGREDIENTS | YIELDS 6 ENCHILADAS

1 tablespoon butter
¼ cup chopped green onions
1 teaspoon minced garlic
1 (10-ounce) can cream of chicken soup
1 cup light sour cream
2 cups chicken, cooked and shredded
1 cup black beans, drained
1 cup shredded mozzarella cheese
2 medium ripe tomatoes, chopped
6 whole-wheat flour tortillas
¼ cup whole milk (dairy or soy)
1 cup shredded Cheddar cheese

1. Preheat oven to 350°F. Lightly grease a 9" × 13" baking dish.

2. In a medium saucepan, melt butter and sauté green onions and garlic until tender.

3. Add cream of chicken soup and sour cream. Heat all and mix together well.

4. Remove ¾ of sauce from pan and set aside. To the remaining ¼ in the pan, add chicken, black beans, mozzarella cheese, and tomatoes. Stir to combine.

5. Fill each whole-wheat tortilla with the chicken mixture and roll up. Place seam-side down in the prepared baking dish.

6. In a small bowl, combine the reserved ¾ of the sauce with the milk. Spoon this mixture over the rolled tortillas and top with Cheddar cheese.

7. Bake for 30–40 minutes until cheese is bubbly.

Taco Dinner

This recipe has very little spice to it since it is geared toward toddlers. To make this recipe acceptable for the whole family, pull your toddler's portion of meat and corn out of the skillet, then add your taco seasoning or green onions to the remaining meat.

INGREDIENTS | YIELDS 12 TACOS

1 pound lean ground beef
1 cup frozen corn, thawed
12 corn taco shells
2 cups shredded green cabbage
1 cup shredded Cheddar cheese
1 cup diced tomatoes

1. In a medium skillet over medium heat, brown ground beef and drain.
2. Return beef to skillet and add corn.
3. Heat corn taco shells according to package directions in the oven.
4. Once shells are crisp, top each one with beef and corn mixture, shredded cabbage, Cheddar cheese, and tomatoes.

Forget Taco Seasoning Packets

Make your own! Mix the following: 1 tablespoon chili powder; ¼ teaspoon each of garlic powder, onion powder, crushed red pepper flakes, and dried oregano; ½ teaspoon each of ground cumin and paprika; and 1 teaspoon each of sea salt and black pepper.

Green Boats

Green boats are a fun way to introduce celery. Get creative and let your children "race" these boats around their plate and across the finish line into their mouths!

INGREDIENTS | YIELDS 8–12 BOATS

4 washed celery stalks
1 (8-ounce) package vegetable cream cheese
Paprika seasoning
Cheddar cheese slices, cut into triangles

1. Cut celery stalks into 4" pieces.
2. Spoon 2 tablespoons of cream cheese into celery and level with a knife.
3. Sprinkle lightly with paprika.
4. Top each with a Cheddar cheese "sail."
5. Cover, chill, and serve.

Eggy Boats

Egg yolks naturally contain vitamin D.

INGREDIENTS | YIELDS 25 BOATS

25 pea pods
6 extra-large hard-boiled free-range eggs
¼ cup Vegenaise or light mayonnaise
2 tablespoons butternut squash purée
¼ teaspoon salt and black pepper, or to taste
½ cup black or green olive slices

1. Wash pea pods and dry thoroughly.
2. Slice the top of the pea pod (the straight side) open to make "pea pod boats."
3. Mash hard-boiled eggs with a fork and mix with Veganaise (or mayonnaise) and butternut squash.
4. Add salt and pepper to taste.
5. Spoon 1 tablespoon into each pea pod and top with olive slices as "lifesavers."
6. Cover, chill, and serve.

Caribbean Dream Boats

These are a great snack! Celery is 95 percent water but also provides fiber, folate, and potassium in one little powerhouse vegetable. It is a great vehicle for your toddler's spreads and dips.

INGREDIENTS | YIELDS 8–12 BOATS

4 washed celery stalks
1 (8-ounce) package light cream cheese (dairy or soy)
1 (8-ounce) can crushed pineapple, drained
¼ cup shredded coconut
Tropical drink umbrellas

1. Cut celery stalks into 4" pieces.
2. Combine cream cheese and pineapple in a bowl.
3. Spoon 2 tablespoons of the cream cheese mixture into celery and level with a knife.
4. Sprinkle lightly with coconut.
5. Top each with a tropical drink umbrella.
6. Cover, chill, and serve.

Mix It Up!

Creativity goes a long way with children. Have fun making different arrangements with their food to tempt them to try new things. Make faces on pizzas or tortillas with vegetables or make a "scene" with their whole plate. Let your children create art with their food, and then watch them eat it!

Zucchini Yachts

This recipe makes a great dish for a group. Serve it with Green Boats, Eggy Boats, and Caribbean Dream Boats (all in this chapter) and have a boat parade for your children!

INGREDIENTS | YIELDS 2 YACHTS

1 medium zucchini
1 medium summer yellow squash, chopped
¼ red onion, chopped
1 medium ripe mango
½ cup finely chopped cilantro
2 tablespoons red wine vinegar
1 tablespoon olive oil

1. Slice zucchini lengthwise to form 2 long boats.

2. Scrape out shallow middle of the zucchini to form the hull of the boat.

3. In a medium bowl, combine yellow squash, onion, mango, and cilantro with red wine vinegar and olive oil until coated thoroughly.

4. Fill the zucchini boats with this mixture.

5. Serve on a slice of romaine lettuce for the "water."

Zucchini Vessels

Hollowed-out zucchinis make great vessels to hold different foods. Fill the zucchini with egg salad, chicken salad, or a fruit salad. Nutritionally, your children will get small amounts of folate, potassium, vitamin A, and manganese when eating zucchini.

Limeade Sorbet

Although grapes are a choking hazard for children under 3, blending them into the limeade makes their sweetness safe and accessible.

INGREDIENTS | YIELDS 2¼ CUPS

1½ cups prepared limeade from frozen concentrate
¾ cup frozen white grapes

1. Combine limeade and frozen grapes in a blender. Blend all ingredients until smooth.

2. Pour into a freezer-safe container.

3. Freeze for 2 hours, then fluff with a fork.

4. Return to freezer.

5. Continue fluffing every 1½–2 hours until serving.

Make Your Own Limeade or Lemonade

Limeade, and its more popular sister, lemonade, are made from mixing the juice of either limes or lemons with white grape juice and agave nectar. Different proportions yield sweeter or tarter results, but try this recipe for a starting place: ¼ cup lime or lemon juice, 2 cups white grape juice, and 1 teaspoon agave nectar. Combine all ingredients and stir. Serve over ice.

Yogurt Applesauce Dip

This dip works well for all kinds of fruit or animal crackers.

INGREDIENTS | YIELDS 2 TABLESPOONS

1 tablespoon applesauce
1 tablespoon vanilla yogurt
¼ teaspoon ground cinnamon

Combine all ingredients and stir well.

Fresh Fruit Slush

This tangy mixture can be used as a light dip for fruit or can be used a dressing to drizzle over fresh fruit. Frozen mangos and strawberries can also be used together as an alternative to peaches.

INGREDIENTS | YIELDS 3 CUPS

1 (10-ounce) package frozen unsweetened peach slices, thawed
1 (10-ounce) package frozen unsweetened sliced strawberries, thawed
2 tablespoons light agave nectar
1 tablespoon lemon juice
1 teaspoon lime juice
¼ teaspoon vanilla extract

1. Combine the all the ingredients in a food processor.
2. Process until smooth.

Chocolate Pomegranate Dip

Pomegranates are also a delicious source of potassium, vitamin C, and fiber. Many children who do not eat five servings of fruit or vegetables per day do not get enough potassium.

INGREDIENTS | YIELDS 3 CUPS

1 small package all-natural instant chocolate pudding
1½ cups whole milk (dairy or soy)
1 cup light sour cream
⅓ cup pomegranate juice
½ teaspoon orange zest

1. In a medium mixing bowl, combine chocolate pudding and milk with a beater. Once blended well, add remaining ingredients and blend until smooth.
2. Chill and serve.

Pomegranate—an Antioxidant Powerhouse

Research shows that commercial pomegranate juice has three times the antioxidant activity as red wine and green tea. Antioxidants have been shown to help in the prevention of cancer and heart disease. Try to incorporate pomegranate juice into your children's diets. Once they are older than four years old and less likely to choke, you can serve them pomegranate fruit.

APPENDIX A

Weekly Organic Menus for Each Age Group

Four to Six Months Menus

Breast Milk or Formula: 24 to 32 ounces per day

Day 1 to 4
Baby's First Rice Cereal
***Watch for signs of allergies for 4 to 7 days and then introduce a new food.

Day 5 to 8
Baby's First Rice Cereal
Apple Purée
***Watch for signs of allergies for 4 to 7 days and then introduce a new food.

Day 8 to 12
Baby's First Rice Cereal mixed with Apple Purée
Apricot Purée
***Watch for signs of allergies for 4 to 7 days and then introduce a new food.

Six to Nine Months Menus

Always introduce new foods separately to watch for signs of allergies. Once your baby has shown no reaction to the foods alone, you can introduce mixtures of foods.

Every Day
Breast Milk or Formula: 24 to 32 ounces per day
Iron-Fortified Infant Cereal: ¼ cup per day

Monday
Rice Cereal
Black Bean Mash
Apricot Pear Purée

Tuesday
Rice Cereal
Pumpkin Peach Oatmeal Cereal
Spinach and Potato Purée

Wednesday
Rice Cereal
Potato and Plum Purée
Peach Raspberry Purée

Thursday
Rice Cereal
Sweet Potato and Carrot Purée
Chicken and Parsnip Purée

Friday
Rice Cereal
Refried Pinto Beans
Fall Harvest Purée

Saturday
Rice Cereal
Apple and Carrot Mash
Chicken, Papaya, and Nutmeg
Mash

Sunday
Rice Cereal
Rutabaga and Pear Purée
Beef and Barley

Nine to Twelve Months Menus

Every Day
Breast Milk or Formula: 24 to 32
ounces per day

Monday
Blueberry Mini Muffins
Lentil Soup
Quinoa and Tofu Bites

Tuesday
Yogurt Berry Parfait
Organic Farmer's Pie
Whole-Wheat Shells with Marinara
Sauce

Wednesday
Oatmeal with Sautéed Plantains
Chickpea, Carrot, and Cauliflower
Mash
Turkey Chili

Thursday
Whole-Grain Waffles with Blue-
berry Syrup
Split Pea Curry
Roast Lamb, Rice, and Tomato
Compote

Friday
Oatmeal with Cinnamon Apples
Cauliflower and Potato Mash
Couscous with Grated Zucchini
and Carrots
Hummus

Saturday
Zucchini Corn Muffins
Lentils with Spinach and Quinoa
Black Bean and Carrot Mash and
Mango and Brown Rice

Sunday
Banana Bread
Vegetable Rice Soup
Vegetable Barley Casserole and
Mashed Sweet Potatoes

Twelve to Eighteen Months Menus

Every Day
Whole milk (dairy or soy): 16
ounces per day
Typical Pattern: 3 meals plus 1 to
3 snacks

Monday
Zucchini Corn Muffins with scram-
bled eggs
Creamy Pasta Salad
Lentils and Brown Rice
Snack: Mangosteen Cereal Mix

Tuesday
Maple Barley Breakfast with whole
milk (dairy or soy)
Broccoli Cheese Soup and whole-
wheat crackers
Baked Honey Pescado with Lem-
ony Rice and Asparagus Salad
Snack: Fruit Kabobs

Wednesday

French Toast with side of fresh fruit

Easy Baked Chicken and Honeyed Carrots

Broccoli with Meat and Rigatoni

Snack: Tropical Pudding Pie Dip with organic vanilla wafers or fresh fruit

Thursday

Spicy Pumpkin Muffins and 6 ounces yogurt (dairy or soy)

Chicken Salad and whole-wheat crackers

Spaghetti Squash with Italian Herbs

Snack: Take-Along Cereal Snack

Friday

Cantaloupe Papaya Smoothie

Chicken Pot Pie Muffins

Macaroni and Cheese with side of steamed broccoli

Snack: Creamy Salsa Dip with blue corn tortilla chips

Saturday

Blueberry Pancakes

Mushroom Barley Casserole

Vegetable Tofu Pot Pie and Creamy Cauliflower Soup

Snack: Pink Milk

Sunday

Spinach Tomato Scramble with slice whole-wheat toast

Roasted Potato Salad and Turkey Divan Muffins

Caribbean Baked Risotto

Snack: Vanilla and Raspberry Sorbet

Eighteen Months and Beyond Menus

Every Day

Whole milk (dairy or soy): 16 ounces per day

Typical Pattern: 3 meals plus 1 to 3 snacks

Monday

Breakfast Burrito

Pumpkin Risotto

Hummus and Mango Sandwich with side of Cucumber Tomato Salad

Snack: Green Boats

Tuesday

Blueberry and Banana Yogurt with Crispy rice

Bean and Avocado Quesadilla

Barbecue Meatloaf Muffins and Frosted Cauliflower

Snack: Caribbean Dream Boat

Wednesday

Mixed Fruit Yogurt Smoothie

Grilled Cheese with Squash and Corn Purée with side of steamed peas

Tabouli Salad and Hummus Yogurt Dipping Sauce with Baked Pita Chips

Snack: Yogurt Applesauce Dip

Thursday

Sweet Potato Biscuits and vegetarian sausage

Taco Dinner

Chicken and Udon Noodles with Roasted Carrots

Snack: Limeade Sorbet

Friday

Sweet Sunflower Seed Butter Dip and Banana Smoothie

Mixed Vegetable Stir-Fry and brown rice

Barbecue Chicken Pizza

Snack: Eggy Boats

Saturday

Cherry Apple Coconut Rice Pudding

Cheesy Polenta with Roasted Vegetables

Quinoa Primavera with grilled chicken or tofu

Snack: Chocolate Pomegranate Dip with fresh berries

Sunday

Raspberry Strawberry Muffins and 6 ounces yogurt

Mango Coleslaw and Pinto Bean Roll-Ups

Black Bean Cakes with Pineapple Salsa

Snack: Mixed Fruit Yogurt Smoothie

Resources

Organic food is becoming more readily available. Most large grocery stores, including Target and Walmart, now carry some organic options. The Internet is also a great resource for learning more about organics, finding farmers' markets and CSAs, and connecting with other people who are interested in pursuing an organic lifestyle.

These are just a few ideas to get you started in learning about how to best provide a balanced, organic diet for your baby and toddler. Other resources include your local chamber of commerce, local hospital, parent support groups, and your local health-food store or grocery store. Once you start looking, you'll see that information on organics is all around you!

Organic Information

The National Organic Program
www.ams.usda.gov/NOP

The Organic Trade Association
www.ota.com

The Organic Trade Association's O'Mama Report
www.theorganicreport.com

The Environmental Working Group
www.foodnews.org

Organic Consumers Association
www.organicconsumers.org

Farmers' Market and Organic Store Finder

Organic.org
www.organic.org

The Alternative Farming Systems Information Center
http://afsic.nal.usda.gov

Pick Your Own Fruits and Vegetables
www.pickyourown.org

Nutrition and Medical Information

Breastfeeding support through La Leche League
www.llli.org

Books about Child Nutrition by Ellyn Satter
www.ellynsatter.com

American Academy of Pediatrics
www.aap.org

Food Allergy and Anaphylaxis Network
www.foodallergy.org

APPENDIX C

Nutritional Information for Common Baby Foods

The number of calories that a baby or toddler needs to stay healthy depends on your child's individual metabolism, how active she is, and how quickly she is growing. In general, you can figure out how many calories per day your child should be eating based on either her weight (for less than 12 months) or her height (for ages 1–3 years).

For infants, the basic calorie requirement is about 50 calories per pound. Of course, if your baby is growing particularly fast, he might need more food—some babies need as few as 35 calories per pound or as many as 75 calories per pound. As long as his height and weight are increasing and are following his particular curve on a growth chart, you don't need to worry. Remember that breast milk or iron-fortified formula will remain your child's primary source of nutrition in his first year—solid foods are just a supplement.

The phenomenal growth of your baby's first year will slow down once she hits the toddler years, and her calorie requirements also begin to slow down. The average toddler needs about 40 calories per day for every inch of height. In addition to calories, your child will also need the required amounts of other vitamins and minerals to stay healthy. Providing a multivitamin is certainly an option, but most vitamins are absorbed best from natural sources. The following list details the vitamins and other nutrients found in a number of fruits, vegetables, and other foods liked by many babies. Experiment and find your child's favorites!

Acorn Squash	
Typical serving size	½ cup
Calories	75
Potassium	450 mg
Vitamin A	450 IU
Vitamin C	12 mg
Dietary Fiber	3.2 g

Apples	
Typical serving size	½ medium
Calories	50
Potassium	79 mg
Vitamin A	37 IU
Vitamin C	3 mg
Dietary Fiber	1.7 g

Avocados	
Typical serving size	¼ cup
Calories	60
Potassium	110 mg
Vitamin A	25 IU
Vitamin C	1 mg
Dietary Fiber	1.8 g

Brown Rice	
Serving size	⅛ cup dry
Calories	85
Potassium	50 mg
Vitamin A	0
Vitamin C	0
Dietary Fiber	1 g

Carrots	
Typical serving size	¼ cup cooked
Calories	15
Potassium	115 mg
Vitamin A	7350 IU
Vitamin C	6 mg
Dietary Fiber	1.5 g

Corn	
Typical serving size	¼ cup
Calories	45
Potassium	115 mg
Vitamin A	1 IU
Vitamin C	3 mg
Dietary Fiber	1.1 g

Green Beans	
Typical serving size	¼ cup cooked
Calories	12
Potassium	65 mg
Vitamin A	200 IU
Vitamin C	3 mg
Dietary Fiber	1 g

Oatmeal	
Typical serving size	¼ cup dry
Calories	60
Potassium	50 mg
Vitamin A	0
Vitamin C	0
Dietary Fiber	1 g

Pasta, Enriched	
Typical serving size	⅛ cup dry
Calories	55
Potassium	0
Vitamin A	0
Vitamin C	0
Dietary Fiber	0.5 g

Peaches	
Typical serving size	½ medium
Calories	25
Potassium	94 mg
Vitamin A	100 IU
Vitamin C	4 mg
Dietary Fiber	1 g

Pearl Barley	
Typical serving size	⅛ cup dry
Calories	90
Potassium	36 mg
Vitamin A	0
Vitamin C	0
Dietary Fiber	4 g

Pears	
Typical serving size	½ medium
Calories	48
Potassium	100 mg
Vitamin A	23 IU
Vitamin C	3 mg
Dietary Fiber	2.5 g

Peas	
Typical serving size	¼ cup cooked
Calories	11
Potassium	45 mg
Vitamin A	500 IU
Vitamin C	21 mg
Dietary Fiber	1.3 g

Plums	
Typical serving size	½ medium
Calories	20
Potassium	90 mg
Vitamin A	350 IU
Vitamin C	4 mg
Dietary Fiber	1 g

Spinach	
Typical serving size	¼ cup
Calories	12
Potassium	248 mg
Vitamin A	4710 IU
Vitamin C	4 mg
Dietary Fiber	1.1 g

Sweet Potatoes	
Typical serving size	¼ cup
Calories	45
Potassium	190 mg
Vitamin A	8100 IU
Vitamin C	6.1 mg
Dietary Fiber	1.8 g

Glossary of
Basic Cooking Terms

Active dry yeast
This is a small plant that has been preserved by drying. When rehydrated, the yeast activates and begins producing carbon dioxide and alcohols.

Al dente
A term used in Italian cooking that refers to the texture of cooked pasta. When cooked "al dente," the pasta is tender, but still firm in the middle. The term literally means "to the tooth."

Bake
To cook in dry heat, usually in an oven, until proteins denature, starches gelatinize, and water evaporates to form a structure.

Beat
To combine two mixtures and to incorporate air by manipulating with a spoon or an electric mixer until fluffy.

Blanch
A means of cooking food by immersing it in boiling water. After blanching, the cooked food is immediately placed in cold water to stop the cooking process. Always drain blanched foods thoroughly before adding to a dish.

Butter
A natural fat obtained by churning heavy cream to consolidate and remove some of the butterfat.

Calorie
A unit of measurement in nutrition, a calorie is the amount of energy needed to raise the temperature of 1 gram of water by 1 degree Celsius. The number of calories in a food is measured by chemically analyzing the food.

Cholesterol
Cholesterol is not a fat, but a sterol, an alcohol and fatty acid, a soft, waxy substance used by your body to make hormones. Your body makes cholesterol and you eat foods containing cholesterol. Only animal fats have cholesterol.

Chop
Cutting food into small pieces. While chopped food doesn't need to be perfectly uniform, the pieces should be roughly the same size.

Confectioner's sugar
This sugar is finely ground and mixed with cornstarch to prevent lumping; it is used mostly in icings and frostings. It is also known as powdered sugar and 10X sugar.

Corn oil

An oil obtained from the germ of the corn kernel. It has a high smoke point and contains a small amount of artificial trans fat.

Cornmeal

Coarsely ground corn, used to make polenta, also to coat foods to make a crisp crust.

Cornstarch

Very finely ground powder made from the starch in the endosperm of corn; used as a thickener.

Deep-fry

To fry in a large amount of oil or melted shortening, lard, or butter so the food is completely covered. In this dry-heat method of cooking, about 10 percent of the fat is absorbed into the food.

Dice

Cutting food into small cubes, usually ¼ inch in size or less. Unlike chopping, the food should be cut into even-sized pieces.

Dissolve

To immerse a solid in a liquid and heat or manipulate to form a solution in which none of the solid remains.

Drain

Drawing off the liquid from a food. Either a colander (a perforated bowl made of metal or plastic) or paper towels can be used to drain food.

Dredge

To dip a food into another mixture, usually made of flour, bread crumbs, or cheese, to completely coat.

Edamame

The word for edible soybeans, a green pea encased in a pod.

Emulsify

To combine an oil and a liquid, either through manipulation or the addition of another ingredient, so they remain suspended in each other.

Fatty acids

A fatty acid is a long chain of carbon molecules bonded to each other and to hydrogen molecules, attached to an alcohol or glycerol molecule. They are short-chain, medium-chain, and long-chain, always with an even number of carbon molecules.

Flaky

A word describing food texture, usually a pie crust or crust on meat, which breaks apart into flat layers.

Flaxseed

This small oil-rich seed is used primarily to make linseed oil, but is also a valuable source of nutrients like calcium, iron, and omega-3 fatty acids.

Fry

To cook food in hot oil, a dry heat environment.

Gluten

A protein in flour made by combining glutenin and gliadin with a liquid and physical manipulation.

Golden

The color of food when it is browned or quickly sautéed.

HDL

High-density lipoproteins, the "good" type of cholesterol that carries fat away from the bloodstream.

Herbs

The aromatic leafy part of an edible plant; herbs include basil, parsley, chives, thyme, tarragon, oregano, and mint.

Hummus

A combination of puréed chickpeas with garlic, lemon juice, and usually tahini; used as an appetizer or sandwich spread.

Hydrogenation

The process of adding hydrogen molecules to carbon chains in fats and fatty acids.

Italian salad dressing

A dressing made of olive oil and vinegar or lemon juice, combined into an emulsion, usually with herbs like basil, oregano, and thyme.

Jelly

A congealed mixture made from fruit juice, sugar, and pectin.

Julienne

To julienne food (also called matchstick cutting) consists of cutting it into very thin strips about 1½–2 inches long, with a width and thickness of about ⅛ inch. Both meat and vegetables can be julienned.

Kebab

Meats, fruits, and/or vegetables threaded onto skewers, usually barbecued over a wood or coal fire.

Kidney bean

A legume, either white or dark red, used for making chili and soups.

Knead

To manipulate a dough, usually a bread dough, to help develop the gluten in the flour so the bread has the proper texture.

Lard

The fat from pork, used to fry foods and as a substitute for margarine or butter.

LDL

Low-density lipoproteins, the "bad" cholesterol, which carries fat from the liver and intestines to the bloodstream.

Lecithin

A fatty substance that is a natural emulsifier, found in eggs and legumes.

Lipid

Organic molecules insoluble in water, consisting of a chain of hydrophobic carbon and hydrogen molecules and an alcohol or glycerol molecule. They include fats, oil, waxes, steroids, and cholesterol.

Long-chain fatty acids

These fatty acids have 12 to 24 carbon molecules bonded to hydrogen molecules and to a glycerol molecule.

Margarine

A fat made by hydrogenating polyunsaturated oils, colored with yellow food coloring to resemble butter.

Marinate

To coat foods in an acidic liquid or dry mixture to help break down protein bonds and tenderize the food.

Mayonnaise

An emulsification of egg yolks, lemon juice or vinegar, and oil, blended into a thick white creamy dressing.

Meat thermometer

A thermometer specially labeled to read the internal temperature of meat.

Medium-chain fatty acids

These fatty acids have 6 to 12 carbon molecules bonded to each other and to hydrogen molecules. Coconut and palm oils contain these fatty acids and they are used in infant formulas.

Mince

Mincing consists of cutting food into very small pieces. In general, minced food is cut into smaller pieces than chopped food.

Monounsaturated oil

A fatty acid that has two carbons double-bonded to each other, missing two hydrogen molecules. These very stable oils are good for frying, but can have low smoke points. Examples include olive, almond, avocado, canola, and peanut oils.

Mortar and pestle

A mortar is a bowl-shaped tool, sometimes made of stone or marble, and a pestle is the round instrument used to grind ingredients in the mortar.

Mouthfeel

A food science term that describes the action of food in the mouth; descriptors range from gummy to dry to slippery to smooth to chewy to tender.

Nuts

The edible fruit of some trees, consisting of a kernel in a hard shell. Most edible nuts are actually seeds and are a good source of monounsaturated fats.

Omega-3 fatty acids

A polyunsaturated fat named for the position of the first double bond. The body cannot make omega-3 fatty acids; they must be consumed.

Omega-6 fatty acids

A polyunsaturated fat name for the position of the first double bond. Too much of this fatty acid in the body can cause heart disease. Like HDL with LDL cholesterol, works in concert with omega-3 fatty acids.

Organic food

Food that has been grown and processed without pesticides, herbicides, insecticides, fertilizers, artificial coloring, artificial flavoring, or additives.

Pan-fry

To quickly fry in a small amount of oil in a saucepan or skillet.

Polyunsaturated oil

A fatty acid that has more than two carbon molecules double-bonded to each other; it is missing at least four hydrogen molecules. Examples include corn, soybean, safflower, and sunflower oils.

Processed food

Any food that has been manipulated by chemicals or otherwise treated, such as frozen food, canned food, enriched foods, and dehydrated foods.

Rancid

Fats can become rancid over time and through exposure to oxygen. The fats oxidize, or break down, and free radicals form, which then exacerbate the process. Rancid fats smell and taste unpleasant.

Reduction

Quickly boiling or simmering liquid to evaporate the water and concentrate the flavor.

Risotto

An Italian rice dish made by slowly cooking rice in broth, stirring to help release starch that thickens the mixture.

Roast

To cook food at relatively high heat in an oven. This is a dry-cooking method, usually used for vegetables and meats.

Roux

A mixture of flour and oil or fat, cooked until the starches in the flour can absorb liquid. It is used to thicken sauces, from white sauce to gumbo.

Saturated fat

A fatty acid that has no double-bonded carbons, but has all the carbons bonded to hydrogen molecules. Butter, coconut oil, and palm oil are all high in saturated fats.

Sauté

To quickly cook food in a small amount of fat over high heat.

Sear

Quickly browning over high heat before finishing cooking by another method. Searing meat browns the surface and seals in the juices.

Season

To change the flavor of food by adding ingredients like salt, pepper, herbs, and spices.

Short-chain fatty acid

A fat that contains 2 to 6 carbon molecules; examples include lauric and octanoic acids.

Shortening

A partially hydrogenated oil that is solid at room temperature, used to make everything from frostings to cakes to pastries and breads.

Shred

Shredding food consists of cutting it into thin strips that are usually thicker than a julienne cut. Meat, poultry, cabbage, lettuce, and cheese can all be shredded.

Simmer

Simmering food consists of cooking it in liquid at a temperature just below the boiling point.

Smoke point

The temperature at which fats begin to break down under heat. The higher the smoke point, the more stable the fat will be while frying and cooking. Butter's smoke point is 350°F, olive oil 375°F, and refined oils around 440°F.

Spices

Aromatic seasonings from seeds, bark, roots, and stems of edible plants. Spices include cinnamon, cumin, turmeric, ginger, and pepper, among others.

Trans

Latin word means "across," referring to the positioning of the hydrogen molecules on the carbon chain of a fatty acid.

Trans fat

A specific form of fatty acid, where hydrogen molecules are positioned across from each other, in the "trans" position, as opposed to the "cis" position.

Tropical oils

Oils from plants grown in the tropic region; the most common are coconut oil and palm oil. These oils are usually fully saturated and are solid at room temperature.

Unsalted butter

Sometimes known as "sweet butter," this is butter that contains no salt or sodium chloride. It's used for greasing pans, since salt in butter will make batter or dough stick.

Unsaturated fat

Fatty acids that have two more carbon molecules double-bonded to each other; an unsaturated fat is missing at least two hydrogen molecules.

Vanilla

The highly aromatic seeds contained in a long pod, or fruit, of the vanilla plant, a member of the orchid family.

Vegetable oil

Oils made by pressing or chemically extracting lipids from a vegetable source, whether seeds, nuts, or fruits of a plant.

Vitamins

Molecules that are used to promote and facilitate chemical reactions in the body. Most vitamins must be ingested as your body cannot make them.

Standard U.S./Metric Measurement Conversions

VOLUME CONVERSIONS	
U.S. Volume Measure	**Metric Equivalent**
⅛ teaspoon	0.5 milliliters
¼ teaspoon	1 milliliters
½ teaspoon	2 milliliters
1 teaspoon	5 milliliters
½ tablespoon	7 milliliters
1 tablespoon (3 teaspoons)	15 milliliters
2 tablespoons (1 fluid ounce)	30 milliliters
¼ cup (4 tablespoons)	60 milliliters
⅓ cup	80 milliliters
½ cup (4 fluid ounces)	125 milliliters
⅔ cup	160 milliliters
¾ cup (6 fluid ounces)	180 milliliters
1 cup (16 tablespoons)	250 milliliters
1 pint (2 cups)	500 milliliters
1 quart (4 cups)	1 liter (about)
WEIGHT CONVERSIONS	
U.S. Weight Measure	**Metric Equivalent**
½ ounce	15 grams
1 ounce	30 grams
2 ounces	60 grams
3 ounces	85 grams
¼ pound (4 ounces)	115 grams
½ pound (8 ounces)	225 grams
¾ pound (12 ounces)	340 grams
1 pound (16 ounces)	454 grams

OVEN TEMPERATURE CONVERSIONS

Degrees Fahrenheit	Degrees Celsius
200 degrees F	95 degrees C
250 degrees F	120 degrees C
275 degrees F	135 degrees C
300 degrees F	150 degrees C
325 degrees F	160 degrees C
350 degrees F	180 degrees C
375 degrees F	190 degrees C
400 degrees F	205 degrees C
425 degrees F	220 degrees C
450 degrees F	230 degrees C

BAKING PAN SIZES

U.S.	Metric
8 × 1½ inch round baking pan	20 × 4 cm cake tin
9 × 1½ inch round baking pan	23 × 3.5 cm cake tin
11 × 7 × 1½ inch baking pan	28 × 18 × 4 cm baking tin
13 × 9 × 2 inch baking pan	30 × 20 × 5 cm baking tin
2 quart rectangular baking dish	30 × 20 × 3 cm baking tin
15 × 10 × 2 inch baking pan	38 × 25 × 5 cm baking tin (Swiss roll tin)
9 inch pie plate	22 × 4 or 23 × 4 cm pie plate
7 or 8 inch springform pan	18 or 20 cm springform or loose-bottom cake tin
9 × 5 × 3 inch loaf pan	23 × 13 × 7 cm or 2 lb narrow loaf or pâté tin
1½ quart casserole	1.5 liter casserole
2 quart casserole	2 liter casserole

Index